Fate, Logic, and Time

FATE, LOGIC, AND TIME

by Steven M. Cahn

Resource *Publications*

An imprint of *Wipf and Stock Publishers*
199 West 8th Avenue • Eugene OR 97401

Resource Publications
An imprint of Wipf and Stock Publishers
199 West 8th Avenue, Suite 3
Eugene, Oregon 97401

Fate, Logic, and Time
By Cahn, Steven M.
Copyright©1967 by Cahn, Steven M.
ISBN: 1-59244-642-6
Publication date 4/7/2004
Previously published by Yale University Press, 1967

To my mother and father

Acknowledgments

I wish to acknowledge the guidance and assistance of Richard Taylor, an inspired and inspiring teacher, whose intellectual integrity and infinite patience create the joy of scholarship in his students.

I also wish to thank Mrs. Jane Isay of Yale University Press for her invaluable editorial advice.

Contents

1 What is Fatalism?

"Does man have free will?" This question has been a perennial issue in the history of philosophy. Philosophers from Plato to Austin have examined this question from a seemingly endless number of perspectives, and it still remains a most perplexing and fascinating problem. Indeed, almost every issue of today's professional philosophical journals contains at least one article that purports to shed some light on this problem.

But interest in this question is not limited to philosophers. Jurists, psychologists, historians, religious thinkers, and many others have been vitally concerned with it, for if no man has free will—if it is not within any man's power to perform any actions other than those which he does, in fact, perform—the implications are profound.

Is a man morally responsible for any of his actions if it is not within his power to refrain from any of them? A kleptomaniac is not held morally responsible for stealing, since it is not within his power to refrain from stealing. But if no man has free will and if, consequently, it is not within a man's power to refrain from any of the actions which he performs, then why should anyone be held morally responsible for any of his actions?

Furthermore, if no man is morally responsible for any of his actions, why does anyone ever deserve punishment? Clarence Darrow time and again successfully employed this sort of argument on behalf of clients who admittedly had

committed the crime of which they were accused. For instance, in his defense of Leopold and Loeb, Darrow argued:

> Nature is strong and she is pitiless. She works in her
> own mysterious way, and we are her victims. We have
> not much to do with it ourselves. Nature takes this job
> in hand, and we play our parts. . . . What had this boy
> to do with it? He was not his own father; he was not his
> own mother; he was not his own grandparents. All of
> this was handed to him. He did not surround himself
> with governesses and wealth. He did not make himself.
> And yet he is to be compelled to pay.[1]

What Darrow did not stress was that his argument, if true,
applies to every action of every person. If no man has free
will, it is not entirely accurate to say, "We have not much to
do with it ourselves." In fact, we have nothing to do with it.
We play parts and have absolutely no choice as to which
parts we shall play.

Interest in the problem of free will, however, is not con-
fined solely to the questions of moral and legal responsibility.
If man has free will, then a science of human behavior is not
possible. As B. F. Skinner, a leading exponent of contemporary behavioristic psychology, points out:

> If we are to use the methods of science in the field of
> human affairs, we must assume that behavior is lawful
> and determined. We must expect to discover that what
> a man does is the result of specifiable conditions and
> that once these conditions have been discovered, we
> can anticipate and to some extent determine his ac-
> tions.[2]

1. *Attorney for the Damned,* ed Arthur Weinberg (New York,
1957), pp. 64–65.
2. B. F. Skinner, *Science and Human Behavior* (New York,
1953), p. 6.

Skinner and those who agree that a science of human behavior is possible have spent many years attempting to develop such a science. If man has free will and if, consequently, certain human actions are inherently unpredictable, then the behaviorists are engaged in a hopeless search for "specifiable conditions" which simply do not exist. If I do make certain free decisions, what point is there in trying to discover why I am forced to make these decisions? If the decision is free, I am not forced to make it.

But attempts to predict human behavior have not been limited to individual human actions. It has been argued that historical movements are inherently predictable and that, therefore, a science of history is possible. As Hegel put it, "Spirit, the rational and necessitated will of [the Idea] is and has been the director of the events of the World's History."[3] This same vision of a science of history lies at the heart of Spengler's "venture of predetermining history"[4] and underlies certain interpretations of the Marxian concept of historical materialism.[5] To what extent are such theories compatible with man's free will? If men who try to alter the historical process are in fact engaged in a hopeless struggle against an omnipotent foe, and if the outcome of history is predetermined, it does not seem possible that man has free will. Therefore, to show that man does have free will would seriously weaken the claims of those who propose a science of history.

The problem of free will is also of great interest to religious thinkers. If no man has free will, is God responsible

3. Georg Wilhelm Friedrich Hegel, *The Philosophy of History*, trans. J. Sibree (New York, 1956), p. 8.

4. Oswald Spengler, *The Decline of the West* (New York, 1932), p. 3.

5. An excellent treatment of the deterministic implications of various interpretations of Marx's concept of historical materialism is contained in Sidney Hook's *Toward the Understanding of Karl Marx* (New York, 1933), passim.

for all of the evil actions which men perform? What point is there to the Biblical injunction, "See, I have set before thee life and death, the blessing and the curse; therefore choose life, that thou mayest live,"[6] if no man ever has a real choice as to what actions he will perform? This is, furthermore, not only a problem for traditional religious faiths. Twentieth-century humanism asks a man to attempt to improve the social order in which he lives. What point is there to such a request if a man has no real control over his actions?[7]

These are but a few of the issues which depend upon an answer to the question of whether man has free will. Before proceeding, however, to discuss various answers to this question, it would be well to clarify just what is meant by the term "free will."

A man is free with regard to a specific action A if and only if he has it within his power to perform A and he has it within his power to refrain from A.[8] A man has free will if and only if he is free with regard to some actions.

Given this explication of free will, it would surely seem

6 *The Holy Scriptures* (Philadelphia, 1941), Deuteronomy, chap. 30, verse 19.

7. It might be argued that such a request is intended to be itself a determining factor in a man's compelled behavior, but this is hardly consistent with the usual interpretations of twentieth-century humanism.

8. The phrase "within his power" is used here in the sense outlined by Richard Taylor in his much-discussed article "I Can," which originally appeared in *The Philosophical Review, 69* (1960), 78–89, and is reprinted in Sidney Morgenbesser and James Walsh, eds., *Free Will* (Englewood Cliffs, N.J., 1962), pp. 81–90. According to Taylor, "within his power" is "a philosophically baffling expression which no one can ever analyze; yet it is something that is well understood." To have an action within one's power entails at least that nothing causes one to perform the action and nothing causes one to refrain from the action. This is not to say, however, that the action is inexplicable. It is simply up to the person himself whether he performs it.

clear that man does have free will. For instance, it would seem obvious that it is now within my power to move my finger to the right and it is also now within my power to move my finger to the left, though I cannot do both at once. If no man has free will, it follows that at this moment either I cannot move my finger to the right or I cannot move my finger to the left, and this is surely an implausible claim.

Furthermore, nothing would seem to be more obvious than that a man sometimes deliberates as to what he will do. He weighs one alternative against another. Two or more courses of action are open to him. He may do one thing and he may do something else. What he does depends on the outcome of his deliberation. Is it possible that no man can ever engage in real deliberation about anything? Is life so arranged that we are mere puppets pulled about by circumstances entirely beyond our control? This is surely a radical and doubtful thesis, and yet many seemingly plausible arguments have been presented to support it.

One such argument depends on the assumption that every event has a cause and that given the cause, the event cannot but occur. Since my decision to perform a certain action A is merely one link in a chain of causation which extends back beyond my birth, it is not up to me whether I make that decision, and it is, therefore, not up to me whether I perform A. This argument can, of course, be generalized so as to apply to all human actions, and it would seem to follow that no human action is free. It is this sort of argument which Hobbes employed to reach his materialistic conclusion that "life is but a motion of limbs."[9]

Another argument against man's free will depends on the assumption that a man must always choose that action which he believes to be best. As Socrates put it, "since there is no one who desires to be miserable, there is no one . . . who

9. Thomas Hobbes, *Leviathan* (London, 1940), The Introduction, p. 1.

6 FATE, LOGIC, AND TIME

desires evil."[10] It was this assumption which led to the Socratic doctrine that virtue is knowledge. If a man knows what is good, he will necessarily seek it. But if this assumption is true, a man cannot avoid making the choices which he does, in fact, make, for if he were able to make other choices, he would be able to choose what he does not believe to be best, and this is, on the Socratic assumption, impossible.[11]

A further argument against man's free will has been developed in the light of modern psychiatry. This argument depends on the assumption that a man's conscious decisions are determined by subconscious factors over which he has no control. Given such factors, the choices which a man makes are the only ones which he can make, for these choices are the result of uncontrollable subconscious factors. As John Hospers puts it:

> A man is faced by a choice: shall he kill another person or not? Moralists would say, here is a free choice— the result of deliberation, an action consciously entered into. And yet, though the agent himself does not know it, and has no awareness of the forces that are at work within him, his choice is already determined for him: his conscious will is only an instrument, a slave, in the hands of a deep unconscious motivation which determines his action.[12]

In other words, since our conscious choices are entirely determined by subconscious forces which are entirely be-

10 Plato, *Meno,* trans Benjamin Jowett (New York, 1957), 78 a–b.

11. For this argument to be used to prove that no man has free will, it is also necessary to assume that what a man believes to be best is not up to him.

12. John. Hospers, "Psychoanalysis and Free-Will," in Wilfrid Sellars and John Hospers, eds., *Readings in Ethical Theory* (New York, 1952), pp. 564–65.

yond our control, it follows that our conscious choices themselves are entirely beyond our control.

All these arguments against man's free will have seemed convincing to many thinkers. However, they are all open to one vital objection: the premise of each argument can be reasonably denied. It can be reasonably denied that every event has a cause, or that a man must always choose what he believes to be best, or that a man's subconscious always controls his conscious decisions. Though each of these premises may seem plausible at first, it could be reasonably maintained that it is more plausible that man has free will than that any of these premises is true.

For instance, suppose it is argued that since every event has a cause no man is free. One could assert that since man is free, not every event has a cause. And this reply is equally as strong as the original argument, since a belief in man's free will is surely as plausible as a belief in the fact that every event has a cause.

In order to prove any proposition P, one must adopt premises from which P can be deduced, such that more evidence exists in support of the premises than in support of the denial of P. If more evidence exists in support of the denial of P than in support of the premises, one can simply deny P and deny the premises.

For instance, suppose that someone claims that life exists on Mars, and that since such life wishes to communicate with people on earth, it is sending out electrical impulses which our scientific equipment can pick up. It follows from this that we should be receiving electrical impulses from Mars. Let us grant the correctness of this reasoning. We are not sure as to the truth or falsity of the premises. However, all available scientific evidence confirms that no electrical impulses are being received from Mars. Here is a case in which more evidence exists in support of the denial of the proposition to be proved than in support of the premises. Thus, one would reply to this argument intended to prove that we are receiving electrical impulses from Mars by simply asserting that since the denial of the conclusion is more plausible than the premises, one denies both the conclusion and the premises.

Any proposition can be "proven" if one adopts suitable premises. The difficulty in any proof is to find premises which yield the desired conclusion and which are more plausible than the denial of that conclusion. Thus, to return to the problem of free will, it is clear that in order to prove that no man has free will, the premises adopted must be very plausible indeed, for the belief that man does have free will is itself very plausible.

Considerations such as these have led philosophers to wonder whether there exist any premises which imply that no man has free will and which are even more plausible than the belief that man does have free will. There is at least one belief which seems even more plausible than the belief that man does have free will: a belief in the laws of logic. Few people wish to deny the law of contradiction, the law of excluded middle, *modus ponens, modus tollens,* and other basic laws of logic, for these laws seem to be, at the very least, necessary conditions for intelligent discourse. Therefore, if it were possible to prove that no man has free will, using as premises only the laws of logic, the proof would be strong indeed. One could deny it only by denying logic itself.

Fatalism rests on the claim that such a proof is possible. It is this claim, which has intrigued philosophers for centuries, that I intend to examine in the following study.

Fatalism is the thesis that the laws of logic alone suffice to prove that no man has free will, suffice to prove that the only actions which a man can perform are the actions which he does, in fact, perform, and suffice to prove that a man can bring about only those events which do, in fact, occur and can prevent only those events which do not, in fact, occur.

In short, if a man is logical, he must view the future as most of us now view the past. As a man looks back on the past he may regret that certain events occurred, but he can do nothing now to undo or "prevent" the occurrence of any event which did, in fact, occur; he can do nothing now to bring about the occurrence in the past of any event which did not, in fact, occur. As a man looks toward the future, he may hope that certain events will occur, but he can do nothing now to prevent the occurrence of any event which will, in fact, occur and he can do nothing now to bring about the occurrence of any event which will not, in fact, occur. Thus, the fatalist argues, no man can ever engage in real deliberation. A man may believe that he is deliberating between two possible courses of action, but, in reality, only one course of action is open to him. His apparent deliberation is a mere illusion.

This is, indeed, a sorry picture of human life. We are all, according to fatalism, powerless to change our destinies. We *can* only do what we *shall* do, and what we shall do is not up to us. Is it possible that such a conclusion is implied solely by the laws of logic?

Consider the following line of argument which in its general form underlies almost every fatalistic argument devised.[13] It must be either true or false that a specific man M will perform a specific act A at a specific time T. Either M will perform A at T or he will not perform A at T. This seems indisputable, and, indeed, it is but an application of what is called in logic "the law of excluded middle." This law states that any proposition whatever must be either true, or if not true, then false. Either it is true that M will perform A at T, or if it is not true that M will perform A at T, then it must be false that M will perform A at T. Of course, it is possible that no one knows whether or not

13. In what follows I am simply presenting a general line of argument without considering objections to it. A consideration of these objections will be taken up in Chapter 3.

M will perform *A* at *T*. Indeed, there may be so many factors relevant to deciding the question of whether or not *M* will perform *A* at *T* that no man could ever be aware of enough of these factors to decide the question conclusively. But this consideration is irrelevant to the seemingly quite unexceptionable claim that either *M* will perform *A* at *T* or he will not. It may not seem terribly significant to make this claim, but, nevertheless, it seems indubitably to be true.

Let us assume that it is true that *M* will perform *A* at *T*. In that case there is no way *M* can prevent his performing *A* at *T*. He may regret that he will perform *A* at *T;* he may wish that he could do something to prevent it; but since it is true that he will perform *A* at *T*, all his efforts to refrain from *A* at *T* will be in vain.

Let us assume next that it is false that *M* will perform *A* at *T*. In that case there is no way *M* can bring it about that he will perform *A* at *T*. He may regret that he will not perform *A* at *T;* he may wish that he could do something to bring it about that he will perform *A* at *T;* but if it is false that he will perform *A* at *T*, all his efforts to perform *A* at *T* will be in vain.

Surely either it is true that *M* will perform *A* at *T* or it is false that *M* will perform *A* at *T*. But in either case, *M* is not free with regard to performing *A* at *T*, for either it is not within his power to refrain from *A* at *T* or it is not within his power to perform *A* at *T*, and a man is free with regard to a certain action only if it is within his power to perform that action and it is also within his power to refrain from that action.

Now this argument can be generalized so as to apply to any action whatever, thus implying that every action is fated and that we have no control over our own destinies. Thus, a simple law of logic—that any proposition must be either true, or if not true, then false—appears to commit one logically to the view that the future is as fixed as the past, and that just as it is not now within anyone's power to alter what happened in the past, so it is not now within anyone's power to alter what will happen in the future.

At this point, philosophers and laymen alike are inclined to feel that something has gone wrong. Though the argument seems reasonable, it appears to be no more than a logical trick. No one knows how it is done, but everyone is convinced that there must be an explanation. One is thus inclined to say that although it is difficult to see just what it is that is wrong with the fatalist's argument, there certainly is something wrong with it.

Could any philosopher of rank really believe that this sort of fatalistic argument is sound? Could any philosopher of rank really believe that the laws of logic alone carry such dire implications? As a matter of fact, Aristotle, the man who first formalized the laws of logic, seems to have believed that this sort of argument is sound and that the laws of logic carried such implications.[14] Because of this and because he believed in man's free will, Aristotle was led to qualify the laws of logic themselves. He did not consider this sort of proof a trick or a sham; he believed it to be sound and he believed that in order to avoid its conclusion one had to deny the very plausible thesis that every proposition must be either true, or if not true, then false.

Aristotle, furthermore, was not alone in taking this argument seriously. Diodorus Cronus, the Megarian philosopher, achieved great fame by constructing a fatalistic argument which was very similar to the one I have presented.[15] Diodorus, however, unlike Aristotle, did not believe that

14. Just what Aristotle's views were on this question has been a matter of much dispute. However, the interpretation I present and discuss in much greater detail in Chapter 3 has been accepted by most commentators.

15. Just what Diodorus' argument was is not known. However, since the premises and conclusion of the argument are known, various attempts have been made to reconstruct it. These reconstructions are discussed in Chapter 4.

man has free will, and so he felt no need to modify any
of the laws of logic in order to maintain such a view.

Many medieval theologians were deeply concerned with
this same problem and such an eminent philosopher as
William of Ockham, after discussing the problem in great
detail, concluded that he simply did not know how to solve
it. Though not many of the medievals agreed with Aristotle
that the sort of proof I presented above is sound, they took
his opinion very seriously and went to great pains in the
attempt to refute it.

In recent years, however, the almost unanimous opinion
among philosophers has been that Aristotle was badly mistaken in these matters and that, contrary to what he believed,
fatalism is a bogy, an absurd claim that cannot possibly
be justified. Aristotle's views have been referred to as "an
instructive tissue of error,"[16] and fatalism has been referred
to as "a fraud [and a] triviality."[17] It has sometimes been
argued that philosophy is useless, since it never reaches any
generally accepted conclusions. But after reading much of
the philosophical literature of the past fifteen years, one
comes away with at least one conclusion that seems to be
generally agreed upon: fatalism is a dead issue, and Aristotle's views on this question are badly muddled.

It is my contention, however, that, despite the belief of
most contemporary philosophers that the issue of fatalism
has been permanently laid to rest, the major arguments in
support of fatalism have never been refuted: they have
merely been ridiculed, derided, and misunderstood. It is my
contention, furthermore, that, contrary to the belief of most
contemporary philosophers, Aristotle's views on the subject
of fatalism are exceptionally profound. Indeed, Aristotle

16. Donald Williams, "The Sea Fight Tomorrow," in *Structure,
Method and Meaning: Essays in honor of Henry M. Sheffer,* ed. P.
Henle, H. M. Kallen, and S. K. Langer (New York, 1951), p. 290.

17. A. J. Ayer, *The Problem of Knowledge* (London, 1957),
p. 170.

provided us with a subtle answer to a serious question which contemporary philosophy has failed to recognize as a real question.

The significance of the issue of fatalism extends far beyond the admittedly important problem of man's free will. Indeed, a proper answer to the fatalist argument carries profound implications about the nature of time and the nature of logic itself; and both these issues are the very forefront of philosophical inquiry today.

Gilbert Ryle once commented, "No philosopher of the first or second rank has defended fatalism or been at great pains to attack it . . . It is not a burning issue."[18] This statement seems to me erroneous for at least two reasons. First because numerous philosophers of both the first and second rank have been greatly concerned with the issue of fatalism. Second, and this is what this essay sets out to show, fatalism is a burning issue, though most contemporary philosophers refuse to see the flames.

In what follows I intend to set forth the strongest arguments in support of fatalism that I know of. These arguments are in most cases formal reconstructions of arguments presented by other thinkers. In carrying out these reconstructions I shall utilize logical tools and techniques which are admittedly anachronistic. However, my major objective is to set forth the most powerful arguments conceivable in support of fatalism. It is indeed possible that the thinkers whose original arguments I have reconstructed would not have accepted my reconstructions, but this is not my concern. My concern is whether these reconstructed arguments are logically sound—whether these arguments yield the conclusions which they claim to yield.

After setting forth these various arguments I shall discuss and explain why I reject all of the most important objections to them. Finally, I shall point out what I take to be both

18. Gilbert Ryle, *Dilemmas* (Cambridge, 1960), p. 28.

the strengths and weaknesses of the fatalistic position and show some of the important implications to be drawn from a correct appraisement of this position.

One of the major reasons why fatalism has not been considered seriously in the past few decades is that the issue which bothered Aristotle, the Stoics, and the medievals has been entirely overlooked by many contemporary philosophers. They have so defined the term "fatalism" as to make it an absurd thesis which is easily refuted. Before beginning to examine the real issue of fatalism and the various arguments which have been put forth in support of it, I should like to discuss fatalism as it has been interpreted—and misinterpreted—by certain contemporary thinkers.

2 A Modern Misinterpretation of Fatalism

Fatalism as I have defined it is the thesis that the laws of logic alone suffice to prove that no man has free will. Though I have not as yet presented any formal proofs of this thesis, I have indicated that such proofs would depend on showing that if it is true that an event *e* will occur, then there is nothing anyone can do to prevent the occurrence of *e*. This point has been the source of a great deal of confusion about fatalism, for many contemporary philosophers seem entirely to misunderstand the nature of the fatalist's claim.

In order to understand how this confusion arises, let us consider a comment made by Sidney Morgenbesser and James Walsh in the introduction to their anthology, *Free Will*. They note that fatalism "can lead to very great worry indeed: does a man *ever* control his own destiny, will all things turn out as they will no matter *what* he does?"[1] If fatalism is true, this surely implies that a man can never control his own destiny. I cannot control what happens to me, if I cannot bring about the occurrence of any events which will not occur and if I cannot prevent the occurrence of any events which will occur. If the actions which I perform are the only actions which I can perform, then I have no control over what will happen to me in the future. If I had such control—if it were up to me whether or not

1. Sidney Morgenbesser and James Walsh, eds., *Free Will* (Englewood Cliffs, N.J., 1962), p. 1.

a certain event would occur—then it would be within my power to bring about the occurrence of the event, and it would also be within my power to prevent the occurrence of the event. Fatalism, however, is the thesis that no man ever has it within his power both to bring about the occurrence of an event and also to prevent the occurrence of that event.

The second question raised by Morgenbesser and Walsh is this: if fatalism is true "will all things turn out as they will no matter *what* a man does?" Many contemporary philosophers believe that fatalism does imply this. They believe that fatalism implies that if it is true that a person will die in 1970, then he will die in 1970 whether or not he commits suicide in 1968. These philosophers, therefore, believe fatalism to be a fallacious doctrine.

A. J. Ayer, for instance, claims that fatalism makes the mistake of equating "the future will be the same, will be what it will be, no matter what we do" with "it would be the same no matter what we did."[2] Thus, Ayer claims that although it is true that given our present actions the future is unalterable, this is not to say that the future would be the same if we did not perform the actions which we do, in fact, perform. Ayer contends that we do have a certain control over the future, since our present actions do affect the future, and it is this control over the future which Ayer believes that fatalism denies.

A similar point is made by Adolf Grünbaum: "The fatalist says that regardless of what we do, the outcome will be the same . . . The fatalist thinks that if you go into combat, and if 'some bullet has your name on it,' you will be killed no matter what you do."[3] Grünbaum thus believes that fatal-

2. A. J. Ayer, "Fatalism," in *The Concept Of A Person and other essays* (New York, 1963), p. 238.

3. Adolf Grünbaum, "Causality and the Science of Human Behavior," in Herbert Feigl and May Brodbeck, eds., *Readings in the Philosophy of Science* (New York, 1953), p. 772.

ism, which he describes as a "prescientific and primitive doctrine," implies the seemingly absurd conclusion that even if one were to wear an impenetrable bulletproof suit of armor in battle, if it were fated that one would be shot, then one would be shot, and the suit of armor would be of no avail.

A consequence of this interpretation of fatalism is pointed out by the University of California Associates, who dismiss fatalism as "preposterous" on the grounds that according to this thesis, "Man's will is no match for the decrees of fate. It is futile to take measures for his welfare, his health, and his safety, for man is powerless to escape his fate."[4] Thus, fatalism implies that learning how to swim is a useless precaution against drowning, for if it is true that one is going to drown, nothing one can do will prevent it, and if, on the other hand, it is true that one is not going to drown, then there is no need to take precautions against drowning.

This view of fatalism is perhaps best summed up by H. Van Rensselaer Wilson:

> The typical fatalist contends that human effort, human wisdom, human skill, even human stupidity, have no causal continuity with the future. The same future will occur, according to the fatalist, no matter what we human beings know or don't know, do or don't do, seek or shun. Our knowing, doing, and seeking may well have determining causes, he would say, but basically they cannot really have effects—at least, they do not make any real difference in the long run . . . For the fatalist, human beings are helpless, ineffectual nonentities in the causal picture.[5]

4. University of California Associates, "The Freedom of the Will," in Herbert Feigl and Wilfrid Sellars, eds., *Readings in Philosophical Analysis* (New York, 1949), p. 614.

5. H. Van Rensselaer Wilson, "Causal Discontinuity in Fatalism and Indeterminism," *The Journal of Philosophy, 52* (1955), 70–71.

Wilson considers the fatalistic thesis to be "untenable," and this is precisely the conclusion reached by Ayer:

> the answer to the fatalist is that his bogy is a fraud. If his only ground for saying that an event is fated to occur is just that it will occur, or even that someone knows that it will, there is nothing more to his fate than the triviality that what happens at any time happens at that time, or that if a statement is true it is true. His bogy would not be a fraud if he could establish that what happens at one time must be causally independent of what happens at another, and, in particular, that the future must be independent of the present: but this he cannot do.[6]

If fatalism is interpreted in the manner suggested by Ayer, Grünbaum, the University of California Associates, Wilson, and many other contemporary philosophers, then fatalism is not merely false but is, in fact, logically inconsistent.

Consider, for instance, the following example: man M and man P become involved in a violent argument, and M challenges P to a fight. M says that he will be waiting for P at 3 P.M. behind the local tavern. According to the interpretation of fatalism adopted by Ayer and those who agree with him, fatalism asserts that whether P wrestles with M in no way depends on what P does prior to 3 P.M. Fatalism so conceived implies that M might wrestle with P behind the local tavern at 3 P.M. even if P left town immediately before 3 P.M. and was, therefore, not in town at 3 P.M. But, obviously, if P was not in town at 3 P.M., M wrestled behind the local tavern with an opponent who was not there, and this is a logical impossibility.

In order to see this point even more clearly, consider a man R who is a bachelor. Fatalism, according to Ayer's definition, implies that R might be divorced tomorrow even

6. Ayer, *The Problem of Knowledge* (London, 1957), p. 179.

if he does not get married. But it is logically impossible for an unmarried man to be divorced. Fatalism, therefore, according to Ayer's interpretation, implies a logical impossibility and is itself, therefore, a logically inconsistent thesis.

It would be easy at this point to dismiss fatalism, as Ayer does, as a "fraud." Indeed, according to Ayer's interpretation, fatalism is worse than a fraud; it is logically inconsistent. But Ayer's interpretation of fatalism, though convenient, evades the points of controversy associated with this issue by generations of other philosophers, which still merit serious philosophical study.

Utilizing the definition of fatalism as the thesis that the laws of logic alone suffice to prove that no man has free will, we have seen that fatalism implies that no man controls his destiny. But, to return to the second question raised by Morgenbesser and Walsh, if fatalism, as traditionally understood, is true, "will all things turn out as they will no matter *what* a man does?" The question can be interpreted in at least two ways: "Will all things turn out as they will no matter which actions within a man's power he performs?" or "Will all things turn out as they will no matter which logically possible actions a man performs?" To illustrate the difference between these two interpretations, consider the original example concerning M, P, and their scheduled struggle behind the local tavern.

Does fatalism commit one to assert that P would have engaged in the struggle with M at 3 P.M. behind the local tavern (call that action A) no matter which actions within P's power he performed? Assuming that P did, in fact, perform A, fatalism implies that it was never within P's power not to perform A, since fatalism further implies that it is never within a man's power not to perform any action which he does, in fact, perform. Could not P have done something to avoid performing A? Fatalism implies that he could not, since, according to fatalism, one cannot prevent the occurrence of any event which does, in fact,

occur. But, suppose P had left town immediately before
3 P.M. That would have prevented A. But P did not leave
town. Therefore, it was never within his power to do so,
for, according to fatalism, the only actions which are within
a man's power to perform are those which he actually
performs.

Thus, to return to the first version, all things will turn
out as they will no matter which of the actions within a
man's power he performs, since, according to fatalism, the
only actions within a man's power are the ones he does
perform. This may seem a strange doctrine, but fatalism is
a strange doctrine whose truth we have yet to consider.
There is thus far, however, nothing contradictory about the
fatalistic thesis as traditionally understood. It may be false,
but it is not, as it is according to Ayer's interpretation, logically inconsistent.

The next question is whether fatalism, as traditionally
understood, commits us to the second position, that all
things will turn out as they will no matter which logically
possible actions a man performs? Fatalism affirms that if
it is fated that M will wrestle with P at 3 P.M., then nothing
can prevent the occurrence of their struggle at the appointed
place and the appointed time. But this is *not* to say that the
struggle would take place no matter what anyone did. If P
left town immediately before 3 P.M. and was, therefore, not
in town at 3 P.M., the struggle would not take place. This is
admitted by the fatalist. To deny it would be, as we have
seen, tantamount to denying logic itself. A man cannot, by
definition, wrestle an opponent who is not there.

All the fatalist denies is that it is within P's power to
leave town immediately before 3 P.M. According to the
fatalist, if it is fated that M will struggle with P behind the
local tavern at 3 P.M., then it is fated that P will not leave
town immediately before 3 P.M. But this is not to say that
it is *logically* impossible for P to leave town immediately
before 3 P.M. There are many actions which are logically
possible and yet are not within anyone's power to perform:

it is logically possible for a man to run a mile in one minute, but it is not within any man's power to do so.

Fatalism does not, and need not, affirm that the actions which are performed are the only ones which are logically possible. All that fatalism need prove is that the actions which are performed are the only ones which are within anyone's power to perform. Therefore, Ayer is incorrect in asserting that fatalism implies that things "would be the same no matter what we did." Fatalism does imply, however, that things would be the same no matter which of the actions within anyone's power he actually performs. Of course, this is not surprising, since according to fatalism the only actions which are within anyone's power to perform are the actions which he does, in fact, perform.

Grünbaum is similarly in error when he writes that "the fatalist thinks that if you go into combat, and if 'some bullet has your name on it,' you will be killed no matter what you do." According to fatalism, it is logically possible that you might wear an impenetrable bulletproof suit of armor. There is nothing self-contradictory in such an assertion, as there is, for example, in the assertion that you, a mortal man, might live forever. If you were to wear such an impenetrable suit of armor you would not be shot. But, according to the fatalist, if it is fated that you will be shot, it is not within your power to wear a bulletproof suit of armor.

The point made by the University of California Associates that "it is futile to take measures for man's welfare" is not true either. If it is fated that you will not die by drowning, it is not futile to learn how to swim since that knowledge may prevent you from drowning. Of course, if you do learn how to swim, then according to fatalism it was fated that you would learn how to swim. If your ability to swim then saves you from drowning, then according to fatalism it was fated that your ability to swim would save you from drowning. According to fatalism you have no choice as to whether you will drown or not. But this is not to say that your learning how to swim may not save you from drowning.

It may save you, and if it does, in fact, save you, then according to fatalism it was fated to save you.

A similar point was made by the Stoic philosopher Chrysippus, who is "often said to have been the greatest logician of ancient times."[7] He was faced with the following argument:

> If the statement "You will recover from that illness" has been true from all eternity, you will recover whether you call in a doctor or do not; and similarly if the statement "You will recover from that illness" has been false from all eternity, you will not recover whether you call in a doctor or not . . . therefore, there is no point in calling a doctor.[8]

This argument was known in antiquity as the "idle argument," since if one were to accept it, he would be led to a life of total inaction. Chrysippus responded to the "idle argument" in the following way:

> If it is fated that "Laius will have a son Oedipus" it will not be possible for the words "whether Laius mates with a woman or does not" to be added, for the matter is complex and condestinate . . . it is fated both that Laius will lie with a wife and that he will beget Oedipus by her . . . Therefore, all captious arguments of that sort can be refuted in the same way. "You will recover whether you call in a doctor or do not" is captious, for calling in a doctor is just as much fated as recovering.[9]

The "idle argument," answered conclusively by Chrysippus more than two thousand years ago, is still being used to refute fatalism by contemporary philosophers.

7. Benson Mates, *Stoic Logic* (Berkeley, 1961), p. 7.

8. Cicero, *De Fato,* trans. H. Rackham (Cambridge, Mass., 1960), p. 225.

9. Ibid., pp. 225–27.

Wilson's comment concerning fatalism's denial of causal efficacy to human actions is also incorrect. If I decapitate my enemy, he will die. According to the fatalist, if it is fated that I will decapitate my enemy, it is fated that he will die. In other words, if it is not within anyone's power to prevent my decapitating my enemy, then it is not within anyone's power to prevent my enemy from dying as a result. Fatalism does not deny causal efficacy to human actions or for that matter to any sort of events. It is not true that our actions "do not make any real difference in the long run." They do make a difference. Indeed, they are fated to make a difference. But all this means is that no one can prevent their making a difference; it does not mean that they make no difference.

The fatalist need not establish, as Ayer claims he must, "that what happens at one time must be causally independent of what happens at another, and, in particular, that the future must be independent of the present." I agree with Ayer that the fatalist cannot do this, since, as I have shown, it is logically impossible to. But Ayer fails to note that the fatalist, in order to prove his thesis, does not have to show that the actions which a man performs have no consequences for the future.

Thus fatalism, as traditionally interpreted, does not imply either that "the future must be independent of the past" or that all things will "turn out as they will no matter which logically possible actions a man performs." What fatalism, as traditionally interpreted, does imply is that no man has free will and that all things will "turn out as they will no matter which actions within a man's power he performs." Can the fatalist actually prove his thesis that the laws of logic alone suffice to prove that no man has free will? It is this question which is my primary concern in this book, and it is this question to which I now turn.

3 Aristotle and the Problem of Future Contingencies

The most influential arguments put forth in support of fatalism have their source in Chapter ix of Aristotle's *De Interpretatione*. Here Aristotle argues that if *every* proposition[1] must be either true, or if not true, then false (i.e. if the law of excluded middle is true), then it follows that no event is contingent. Because Aristotle is committed to the view that certain events *are* contingent, he is led to assert that there are, in fact, a certain limited class of propositions which are neither true nor false, though any disjunction of such a proposition with its denial is necessarily true. Thus, although Aristotle does not believe that fatalism is true, he does believe that if one is committed to the thesis that every proposition must be true, or if not true, then false, then he is thereby logically committed to the denial of man's free will. It is this belief of Aristotle's which has provoked so much dispute through the centuries, and it is this belief I now propose to discuss.[2]

1. "Proposition" and "statement" are to be taken synonymously throughout this chapter.
2. Although the interpretation of Aristotle which I am presenting has been accepted by most commentators (see, for instance, W. D. Ross, *Aristotle* [New York, 1959], p 82, or Richard Taylor, "The Problem of Future Contingencies," *The Philosophical Review, 66* [1957], 1–28, or I. M. Bochenski, *A History of Formal Logic* [Notre Dame, Indiana, 1961], pp. 62–63, or William Kneale and

The key word in Aristotle's argument is "contingent." What exactly is it for an event to be contingent? An event *e* is contingent if it is not the case that the occurrence of *e* is necessary and it is not the case that the nonoccurrence of *e* is necessary. Contingency is thus defined in terms of necessity. But what is it for an event to be necessary?

An event is necessary if it is not within anyone's power[3] to prevent the occurrence of the event.[4] To prevent an event is to perform some action sufficient for the nonoccurrence of the event. An action is sufficient for the nonoccurrence of an event if the action is logically or physically incompatible with the nonoccurrence of the event. For example, a man's being mortal is logically incompatible with his living forever: it is logically contradictory to assert that a mortal man lives forever. On the other hand, a man's being without oxygen is physically incompatible with his being alive. It is not logically contradictory to assert that

---

Martha Kneale, *The Development of Logic* [Oxford, 1962], pp. 45–54) there are those commentators who do not find this interpretation acceptable (see, for instance, Nicholas Rescher, *Studies in Arabic Logic* [Pittsburgh, 1963], pp. 43–54, or Jaakko Hintikka, "The Once and Future Sea Fight," *The Philosophical Review, 73* [1964], 461–92). However, for the purposes of my discussion, it makes little difference whether Aristotle actually held the views which I am here attributing to him. What is important is the validity of the views themselves. If the reader would feel more comfortable, henceforth in this essay when I refer to "Aristotle's view," the reader may substitute "a commonly accepted interpretation of Aristotle's view."

3. Or within the power of any group of men.

4. It would not in any way weaken Aristotle's arguments if one were to define a "necessary event" more broadly, e.g. as an event which no living being could prevent, or as an event which no inanimate object could prevent, or even as an event which no other event could prevent. However, historically, the arguments have been discussed in terms of man's free will, and so I have chosen to adopt this same procedure. A similar point could be made concerning all of the fatalistic arguments discussed in this essay.

a man lives without oxygen, but it is not a physical possibility for any man to do this.

Thus, Aristotle's view of a necessary event implies neither that a statement denying the occurrence of the event is self-contradictory nor that anyone knows anything whatever about the occurrence or nonoccurrence of the event. Aristotle's view of a necessary event *does* affirm, however, that if an event is necessary, then it is not within anyone's power to prevent the occurrence of that event; similarly, if the nonoccurrence of an event is necessary, it is not within anyone's power to bring about the occurrence of that event. Since fatalism is the thesis that the laws of logic alone suffice to prove that no one has it within his power to prevent any event which does, in fact, occur, if Aristotle proves that the acceptance of the law of excluded middle logically commits one to the necessity of all events, he will have proven that fatalism is true.

Aristotle presents essentially two arguments to support his thesis. Before outlining these two arguments, however, two further modal terms need to be explicated in terms of the notion of "necessity" which has been discussed above. An event *e* is possible if it is not the case that the nonoccurrence of *e* is necessary. An event *e* is impossible if the nonoccurrence of *e* is necessary. Thus, every contingent event is possible, though not every possible event is contingent; for if any event is necessary, it is also possible, though it is not contingent. For example, it is now necessary that Abraham Lincoln was assassinated—it is not now within anyone's power to prevent Lincoln's assassination. From this it follows that the assassination of Lincoln is now possible, for an event is possible if it is not the case that the nonoccurrence of the event is necessary, and since Lincoln's assassination is now necessary, the nonoccurrence of Lincoln's assassination cannot now also be necessary. But although Lincoln's assassination is now possible, it is not now contingent. An event is contingent only if it is not the case that the event is necessary and it is not the case that the non-occurrence of the event is necessary. Since Lincoln's assassination is now necessary, it is not now contingent.

Given these modal notions, let us consider Aristotle's two arguments which are designed to prove that if one is committed to the thesis that every proposition must be true, or if not true, then false, then he is thereby logically committed to the view that all events are necessary, and, therefore, the view that fatalism is true.

ARGUMENT I:

(1) Every proposition must be either true, or if not true, then false.

(2) Assume that one man affirms today that an event of a given character (e.g. a sea-fight) will occur tomorrow and another denies this.

(3) The statement of the one man corresponds with reality and that of the other does not.

(4) But in that case it must already be true that a sea-fight will take place tomorrow, such that there is now no possibility that it might not, or else it must already be true that a sea-fight will not take place tomorrow, such that there is now no possibility that it might.

(5) In either case "nothing is or takes place fortuitously,[5] either in the present or in the future, and there are no real alternatives; everything takes place of necessity and is fixed . . . for the meaning of the word 'fortuitous' in regard to present or future events is that reality is so constituted that it may issue in either of two opposite directions."[6]

5. Aristotle's term "fortuitous" is equivalent to my term "contingent."

6. Aristotle, *De Interpretatione*, 18ᵇ, 5–9. All quotations are from *The Basic Works of Aristotle*, ed. Richard McKeon (New York, 1941).

Note that this argument, as Aristotle himself points out, does not at all depend on anyone actually making such predictions at any time.

ARGUMENT II:

   (1) Every proposition must be either true, or if not true, then false.
   (2) If "a thing is white now, it was true before to say that it would be white, so that of anything that has taken place it was always true to say 'it is' or 'it will be.' "
   (3) "But if it was always true to say that a thing is or will be, it is not possible that it should not be or not be about to be."
   (4) When "a thing cannot not come to be, it is impossible that it should not come to be, and when it is impossible that it should not come to be, it must come to be."
   (5) "All, then, that is about to be must of necessity take place."[7]

It should be carefully observed that Aristotle himself rejects the first premise of each of the above arguments and, therefore, rejects the conclusion of each. But the question at issue is this: assuming the first premise of each argument to be true, are the arguments themselves valid? It is my contention that both these arguments are valid, and in what follows I will defend them against all the important objections I know of.

Let us first examine Argument I. Step (1) and step (2) require no special comment. Step (3), however, is certainly in need of some clarification. Assuming that a sea-fight will take place tomorrow, in what sense does the statement that such a fight will take place correspond with reality?

7. Ibid., 19^a, 9–20.

According to C. A. Baylis, a correspondence theory of truth such as Aristotle's does not require that a fact now exists consisting of the sea-fight's occurrence, but only that a fact will exist at some time in the future consisting of the sea-fight's occurrence. But is there some special problem about future facts which does not also pertain to past facts? Baylis thinks not:

> Consider, for example, a proposition about the past, say the proposition, "Columbus discovered America in 1492." Is it not sufficient for the present truth of this proposition that in 1492 it was a fact that Columbus discovered America? Surely his discovery of America need not be a fact today.[8]

Baylis then implies that the future presents us with no greater difficulties. He seems to be suggesting that if it is true that a sea-fight will take place tomorrow, it is sufficient for the present truth of this proposition that it will be a fact that a sea-fight will take place tomorrow, and that the existence of such a fact tomorrow provides us with no difficulties.

But what does it mean to assert that "it will be a fact that the event e will occur"? Let us first consider what it means to assert that "it was a fact that the event e did occur." What this seems to imply[9] is that (1) the event e occurs, (2) e occurs prior to the present moment, and (3) it is not now within anyone's power to prevent the occurrence of e. Of course, we might now do something which is a sufficient condition for the occurrence of e in the past. For example, my eating lunch with my friend in New York at 12:00 P.M. on July 1, 1965, is sufficient for his having been alive at 11:00 A.M. on July 1, 1965. I can, however, perform only those actions which are sufficient conditions for events which actually took place, for if I could perform actions which are sufficient

8. Charles A. Baylis, "Are Some Propositions Neither True Nor False?" *Philosophy of Science, 3* (1936), 162.
9. This is not intended as a logical analysis.

conditions for events which did not take place, it would be within my power to alter what happened in the past, and that is not the case.

Now, similarly, to assert that "it will be a fact that the event *e* will occur" seems to imply (especially considering the parallel between past and future facts suggested by Baylis himself) that (1) the event *e* occurs, (2) *e* occurs after the present moment, and (3) it is not now within anyone's power to prevent the occurrence of *e*. Of course, we might now do something which is a sufficient condition for the occurrence of *e* in the future. For example, if I am eating lunch with my friend in New York at 12:00 P.M. on July 1, 1965, that is sufficient for his being in the Western hemisphere five seconds later. I can, however, only perform actions which are sufficient conditions for events which will take place, for if I could perform actions which are sufficient conditions for events which will not take place, it would be within my power to alter what will happen in the future, and there is no reason to assume that that is the case. This is not to say that it is not within my power to affect the future, i.e. perform actions which are sufficient conditions for future events, but in that sense I can also affect the past, i.e. perform actions which are sufficient conditions for past events.

Thus, there *is* a problem about future facts, but it is not their futurity, as Baylis suggests, which is bothersome. It is, rather, their factuality. If it is true now that there will be facts consisting of the occurrences of all future events, i.e. if every proposition must be true, or if not true, then false, then it would seem that we can affect the future (and future facts) only as we affect the past (and past facts), i.e. we can perform only those actions which are sufficient conditions for events which actually have occurred or actually will occur. And this is fatalism.

Aristotle, in fact, goes on to make this explicit in step (4) of Argument I. It has been suggested that step (4) is erroneous, since from the truth of a statement that a certain event occurred, it does not follow that the event necessarily occurred. Similarly then, from the truth of a statement that a certain event will occur, it does not follow that the event necessarily will occur. Gilbert Ryle seems to suggest this point when he writes, "Why does the slogan 'Whatever is, always was to be,' seem to imply that nothing can be helped, where the obverse slogan 'Whatever is, will always have been' does not seem to imply this?"[10]

But this objection seems to overlook the relevant sense of "necessity" explicated above. Of course, from the truth of a statement that a certain event occurred, it does not follow that a statement as to the nonoccurrence of the event is contradictory or that anyone must know anything whatever about the occurrence of the event. It does follow, however, that it is not within anyone's power to alter the occurrence of the event, and in the relevant sense of "necessary," the event is necessary. Similarly, from the truth of a statement that a certain event will occur, it does not follow that a statement as to the nonoccurrence of the event is contradictory or that anyone must know anything whatever about the occurrence of the event. It does follow, however, that it is not within anyone's power to alter the occurrence of the event, and, therefore, in the relevant sense of "necessary," the future event is just as necessary as the past event. If we grant step (4), Aristotle seems then to have made his case, since step (5) seems unexceptionable.

Turning next to Argument II, steps (1) and (2) require no special comment. Step (3), however, opens Aristotle up to another objection. Donald Williams remarks that Aristotle is here assuming that *"If there is a sea fight tomorrow, it is necessary that there is a sea fight tomorrow,"* and this is an obvious fallacy, for it implies that every event which occurs is necessary and likewise every event which does not occur is impossible.[11]

10. Ryle, p. 21.
11. Williams, p. 292.

But if it is true that there will be a sea-fight tomorrow, then in the relevant sense of "necessary," it *is* necessary that there will be a sea-fight tomorrow, for if there will be a sea-fight tomorrow, nothing anyone is able to do can prevent it. If one protests that he can do something to prevent the sea-fight tomorrow, though as a matter of fact he will not exercise that ability, it is important to clarify just what sort of ability that person possesses. He may know how to prevent the sea-fight, but given that it *is* going to occur, he is simply not able to exercise his know-how, and in that relevant sense of "ability" he is not able to prevent the sea-fight. If one persists in claiming that in an important sense of "ability," he does have the ability to prevent tomorrow's sea-fight even though it is going to occur, it should be noted that in exactly the same sense of ability, he does have the ability to obviate (or perhaps "postvent"[12]) a sea-fight which took place yesterday, since he also knows just how to obviate that sea-fight (e.g. by reading in an accurate newspaper that no sea-fight took place yesterday). If then it is maintained that one does have the ability (and not merely the know-how) to alter the future, though one does not, in fact, exercise that ability, it should be noted that in exactly the same sense one would seem to have the ability to alter the past, though (and this certainly does sound strange) one does not, in fact, exercise that ability. Thus, if it is true that there will be a sea-fight tomorrow, whatever sort of actions anyone can perform to prevent that sea-fight, he can also perform a similar sort of actions to obviate a sea-fight which took place yesterday.

Of course, it is no argument against Aristotle to simply point out, as Williams does, that Aristotle's arguments lead to the conclusion that every event which occurs is necessary

12. The term "postvent" forms the basis for a provocative essay by Richard Taylor entitled "Prevention, Postvention, and the Will" in Keith Lehrer, ed , *Freedom and Determinism* (New York, 1966), pp. 65–85.

and, likewise, every event which does not occur is impossible, for this is precisely the fatalistic position which Aristotle intended to prove. Aristotle then seems to have made his case, since granted step (3), steps (4) and (5) seem unexceptionable.

If both Argument I and Argument II are sound, how does Aristotle propose to avoid the fatalistic conclusions which both arguments yield? He suggests that "since propositions correspond with facts, it is evident that when in future events there is a real alternative, and a potentiality in contrary directions, the corresponding affirmation and denial have the same character."[13] Thus, Aristotle suggests that if an event is neither necessary nor impossible, but rather contingent, a statement to the effect that the event will occur is neither true nor false. The whole truth is expressed by saying that the event might or might not occur. Nevertheless, a disjunction of a proposition asserting the future occurrence of a contingent event together with the denial of that proposition is necessarily true. A discussion of this latter part of Aristotle's thesis, however, will be postponed until Chapter 7. At this point we have to consider some major objections which have been proposed to Aristotle's view that any proposition which affirms or denies the occurrence of a future contingent event is not true and not false.

According to this view a proposition may change its truth-value.[14] Thus, it may be neither true nor false on September 6, 1948 that a sea-fight occurs on Sept. 7, 1948 ("occurs" to be considered tenselessly),[15] but by Sept. 7 it may be true that a sea-fight occurs on Sept. 7. This would be the case if, for instance, it is up to me on Sept. 6 whether or not a sea-fight takes place on Sept. 7, and on the evening of Sept. 6 I

13. Aristotle, *De Int.*, 19ª, 32–35.

14. For a full discussion of this point and the implications for the nature of time, see Chapter 8.

15. A proposition is true at some specific time t_1 if and only if a person who utters the proposition at t_1 speaks truly.

issue an order which is sufficient for the occurrence of the
sea-fight on Sept. 7.

It has been argued, however, that all temporal references
in propositions are, in principle, eliminable, if replaced by
explicit references to dates. Thus, W. V. O. Quine argues
that "Logical analysis is facilitated by requiring rather that
each *statement* be true once and for all or false once and for
all, independently of time. This can be effected by rendering
verbs tenseless and then resorting to explicit chronological
descriptions when need arises for distinctions of time."[16]
It is this sort of thesis which leads Donald Williams to speak
of "the totality of being, of facts, or of events as spread out
eternally in the dimension of time as well as the dimensions
of space."[17] But, if a proposition such as (1) "Columbus discovered America" could be rendered without loss of meaning as (2) "Columbus discovers America in A.D. 1492"
("discovers" to be understood tenselessly), Aristotle would
be shown to be in error, since the tense of the verb in (1),
which would be eliminable without loss of meaning in (2),
could hardly affect the truth-value of (1).

However, it does *not* seem to be the case that all temporal
references are eliminable in this way.[18] If I do not know
whether A.D. 1492 is before or after the present time, then
I do not know whether Columbus already has discovered
America or whether he has yet to do so, though I do know
that fact given proposition (1). Perhaps then the transforma-
tion of (1) might be (3) "Columbus discovers America and
the time at which he does so is prior to now." Unfortunately,
this merely smuggles in the temporal reference once again,
since unless one is aware of that specific time which is

16. Willard Van Orman Quine, *Elementary Logic* (rev. ed. New
York, 1965), p 6.

17 Williams, p. 282.

18 A clear and concise discussion of this controversy may be
found in Arthur Danto's *Analytical Philosophy of History* (Cambridge, 1965), pp. 198–200.

designated by "now," one would not know when "now" is, since it can designate an infinite number of different times.[19] It thus appears that although the temporal reference in (1) can be shuffled away from the verb and into some date or some adverbial phrase while expressing the verb tenselessly, (1) cannot be so transformed as to eliminate temporal references without a loss of meaning, and thus Aristotle's thesis remains intact.

A second criticism of his thesis is that if certain statements about the future are neither true nor false, why should not certain statements about the past likewise be neither true nor false? Suppose some past event to have been uncaused. Would not a statement as to its occurrence be according to Aristotle, neither true nor false?

But this surely misses the point of Aristotle's remarks. It is not the fact that the occurrence of an event is uncaused which makes that event contingent. An event is contingent only so long as it is within someone's power to bring about the occurrence of the event and it is within someone's power to prevent the occurrence of the event. But this is not the case with regard to any past event. No past event is within someone's power to bring about and within someone's power to prevent. This fact is conveyed simply by the maxim "Don't cry over spilt milk." Whether the past event was caused or uncaused makes no difference in regard to whether the event is now contingent.

On the other hand, a future event may be contingent (i.e. the present situation may be such that it is within someone's power to bring about the occurrence of the event and it is within someone's power to prevent the occurrence of the event). In order to express the whole truth about an event which occurred in the past, we should say that it is true that it did occur. In order to express the whole truth about an

19. For a discussion of the paradoxes generated by the use of "now" without temporal references, see Richard Gale's "Is It Now Now?" *Mind, 73* (1964), 97–105.

event which is a future contingency, we should say that it is neither true that it will occur nor false that it will occur. This does not imply either that the future event will have a cause or that the future event will not have a cause. All this implies is that it is now within someone's power to bring about the event and it is now within someone's power to prevent the event.

A third objection to Aristotle's thesis can be phrased aptly in terms of a wager. Suppose a person P bets that it is true that a sea-fight will take place tomorrow. Assume that when the bet is made the occurrence of the sea-fight is contingent and that when tomorrow arrives the sea-fight actually takes place. P then claims to have been correct, since he bet that a sea-fight would take place, and, in fact, a sea-fight did take place. Is P's claim not justified?

The fact that a sea-fight actually took place does not confirm P's opinion. At best it shows that his opinion became true.[20] When the bet was made it was not true that a sea-fight would not take place, and it was not *yet* true that a sea-fight would take place. It was, in fact, still contingent whether a sea-fight would take place. P's bet that it was true that a sea-fight would take place implied (as Aristotle's Arguments I and II show) that it was not contingent whether a sea-fight would take place, and P was therefore in error.[21]

This last reply, however, leads directly to a fourth objec-

20 Strictly speaking the prediction "a sea-fight will take place tomorrow" does not become true. What does become true is the prediction "a sea-fight takes place on Sept. 7, 1948" ("takes" to be considered tenselessly).

21. Common usage supports Aristotle on this point. Consider a man who bets that horse A will win a particular race. After the race is over and horse B has won, the man who bet on horse A is told that at the time he placed his bet it was true that horse B would win the race. Would not the man immediately suspect that the race was fixed? The winner of a bet is the man whose prediction becomes true, not the man whose prediction was true. P wins his bet but loses the philosophical argument.

tion to Aristotle's position which has been stated by John Turk Saunders thus: "It [Aristotle's theory concerning future contingencies] distorts what we customarily intend by predictions, for we usually mean by these to assert the future occurrence of an event and not to assert (as this theory would suggest) that the event is predetermined."[22] Colin Strang makes a similar point when he distinguishes between a "loaded sense" and a "straight sense" of "it will be."[23] In the former sense, he says, "it will be" implies that the event in question is already causally determined by the present state of affairs, while in the latter sense "it will be" simply means that the event in question "will . . . be present" without this assertion carrying with it any implication as to whether the event in question is already causally determined by the present state of affairs, or whether, in fact, the event has any cause whatsoever.

Charles Hartshorne, who has defended a modified Aristotelian view, replies to Strang in this manner: "Thus my difference from Strang is simply that I reject his 'straight sense' of truth altogether, so far as factual propositions are concerned."[24] But Hartshorne does not really explain why he rejects the "straight sense" of truth, and, thus, he seems merely to be begging the issue. If Aristotle's view is to be upheld, this "straight sense" of truth does, indeed, have to be rejected. Are there any grounds on which it *can* reasonably be rejected? The objection raised by Saunders and Strang can be put succinctly: Is it not possible to assert truly that a contingent event is going to occur tomorrow?

I believe that this question should be answered in the negative. A contingent event is an event which, according to

22. John Turk Saunders, "A Sea Fight Tomorrow?" *The Philosophical Review, 67* (1958), 374.

23. Colin Strang, "Aristotle and the Sea Battle," *Mind, 69* (1960), 463.

24. Charles Hartshorne, "The Meaning of 'Is going to be,' " *Mind, 74* (1965), 55.

the definition given previously, is within someone's power
to bring about and is within someone's power to prevent.
What does it mean then to assert that it is true that such an
event will occur tomorrow? Let us consider a specific example. Assume that it was true yesterday and is true today
that a specific event *e* will take place tomorrow. If *e* is now
a contingent event, then it is now within someone's power
to bring about *e* tomorrow and it is now within someone's
power to prevent *e* tomorrow. Let us consider the latter
possibility. If it was true yesterday that *e* would occur
tomorrow, is it now within someone's power to prevent *e*
tomorrow? Of course, if it was true yesterday that *e* would
occur tomorrow, then no one is going to prevent *e*. But is it
within anyone's power to prevent *e,* even if, by hypothesis,
he does not exercise that power?[25]

Suppose that some person P could prevent *e* tomorrow.
Then, it follows from that that P has it within his power to
render it false that *e* will occur tomorrow. But if P has it
within his power to render it false that *e* will occur tomorrow, then P also has it within his power either (1) to render

25. It would be possible at this point to argue in the following
manner: if it was true yesterday that *e* occurred the day before
yesterday, then no one had it within his power yesterday to prevent
e; similarly then, if it was true yesterday that *e* would occur today,
then no one had it within his power yesterday to prevent *e*. The
challenge is to present a reason for abandoning the latter argument
which is not an equally good reason for abandoning the former
argument, an argument which is clearly valid. If no such reason can
be presented, and I do not believe it can, then it makes no more sense
to argue that "it will be" carries no implication concerning the
necessity of what will be, than that "it was" carries no implication
concerning the necessity of what was (keeping in mind the specific
type of necessity involved here).

I have chosen in the text, however, to utilize a somewhat different
argument against Saunders and Strang. My reasons for this are
(1) the first argument has already been developed and defended in the
chapter and (2) the argument in the text is intuitively stronger and
raises many interesting issues which deserve philosophic airing.

it true and false that *e* will occur tomorrow or (2) to render
false what is true, i.e. to render it false that *e* will occur
tomorrow, whereas, by hypothesis, it is true that *e* will occur
tomorrow. The first option is absurd. No one can render it
true and false that *e* will occur tomorrow, for no one has it
within his power to contravene the law of contradiction. The
second option seems no more reasonable. If P has it within
his power to render it false that *e* will occur tomorrow, then
P has it within his power to alter the past, for he has it within
his power to render it true that a proposition was false,
whereas, by hypothesis, the proposition was true. If it was
true yesterday that *e* would occur tomorrow, this logically
implies that *e* will occur tomorrow. If P can prevent the
occurrence of *e* tomorrow, then P can render it true that it
was not true yesterday that *e* would occur tomorrow. As a
matter of fact, however, it was true yesterday that *e* would
occur tomorrow. Thus, if P can prevent the occurrence of *e*
tomorrow, he can alter the past, and this is absurd.[26]

Since both (1) and (2) are absurd, it is not the case that
anyone has it within his power to prevent *e* tomorrow. But if
no one has it within his power to prevent *e* tomorrow, then *e*
is necessary and cannot be contingent. It is, therefore, a con-

26. Despite the protests of Saunders and Strang I think it clear
that common usage once again supports Aristotle's position. To see
this one need only sketch the fatalist's general line of argument to a
nonphilosopher. His immediate reaction is to reject the assumption
that it is already true or already false that he will perform a certain
action tomorrow. He argues that it may be probable or highly probable that he will perform (or not perform) the action tomorrow,
but it is *not yet* true that he will (or will not) do so. It is only
philosophers who find difficulty with this locution. I do not wish to
argue that common usage proves these philosophers to be wrong.
However, after having discussed this particular question with numerous nonphilosophers, I have been convinced that common usage,
so often cited against Aristotle, provides no evidence against his
view and, in fact, provides a good deal of evidence in support of his
view.

tradition to assert that it is true that a contingent event *e* will occur, for if it is true that *e* will occur, then *e* is not contingent.

This reply, however, raises another objection to Aristotle's thesis, which has been discussed by Martha Kneale. She points out that the use of "was true," "is true," and "will be true" adds no information to the sentences of which they are a part. Thus, "it is true that there will be a sea-fight" is equivalent to "there will be a sea-fight." In other words, "by introducing the phrase 'it is true that' we make no assumption about determinism which is not made by use of the simple sentence in the future tense."[27]

One can agree with Mrs. Kneale's logical point that "it is true that there will be a sea-fight" is equivalent to "there will be a sea-fight." But to speak of the latter sentence as "simple" is surely to beg the issue. I have shown that "it is true that there will be a sea-fight" implies that it is not within anyone's power to prevent a sea-fight. Since "it is true that there will be a sea-fight" is equivalent to "there will be a sea-fight," it follows that "there will be a sea-fight" implies that it is not within anyone's power to prevent a sea-fight.

To consider Mrs. Kneale's point from another viewpoint, if there will be a sea-fight tomorrow, what alternatives do I have in making my "decision" as to whether there will be a sea-fight tomorrow? Of course, one could argue that it is within my power to decide that there will not be a sea-fight tomorrow, though, as a matter of fact, I will not make that decision. This argument, however, is no better than when it was discussed earlier, for in the very same sense of "within my power" it is also within my power to decide that a sea-fight which took place yesterday did not occur, though, as a matter of fact, I will not make that decision.

27. Kneale and Kneale, p. 51. A similar point is made by Friedrich Waismann in "How I See Philosophy," in *Logical Positivism*, ed. A. J. Ayer (Glencoe, 1959), pp. 352–55.

Thus Mrs. Kneale is correct in asserting that the addition of the phrase "it is true that" to a sentence does not change the meaning of the sentence. She is in error, though, in assuming that the truth of a statement such as "There will be a sea-fight tomorrow" carries with it no limitations on anyone's ability to prevent a sea-fight tomorrow.

But this raises yet another objection to Aristotle's theory, for as Gilbert Ryle has remarked, "events themselves cannot be made necessary by truths . . . The fatalist theory tries to endue happenings with the inescapability of the conclusions of valid arguments."[28] Ryle thus seems to be suggesting that the fact that it is true that there will be a sea-fight tomorrow can in no way affect whether there actually will be a sea-fight tomorrow, since a statement is a logically different sort of entity from an event. To take Ryle's own example, if it is true that while I am playing bridge tomorrow I will revoke, that in no sense forces me to revoke, since "A proposition can imply another proposition, but it cannot thrust a card into a player's hand."[29] As Ryle might say in his own well-known terminology, the fatalist is making a category-mistake equivalent to saying that "He tried to flag my cough with a Q.E.D."[30]

Ryle is certainly correct in asserting that propositions do not cause events. However, the truth of a proposition may reflect or describe a state of affairs of the world. Thus, if it is true that I will revoke, this implies that the present state of affairs is so constituted that I will revoke. But if the present state of affairs is so constituted that I will revoke, then, as we have seen, it is no longer within my power not to revoke. In other words the truth of the proposition "I will revoke" does not force me to revoke; however, that proposition describes a state of affairs, an existing set of events, which does

28. Ryle, p. 24.
29. Ibid., p. 22.
30. Ibid., p. 24.

force me to revoke. As Arthur Danto puts it, "a sentence being true is not something which happens, but rather, if a sentence is true, what it is true of must happen."[31] Thus, the assumption that I will revoke is incompatible with it being up to me whether or not I will revoke, and this does not assume either that propositions cause events or, for that matter, that events cause propositions.

A further objection to Aristotle's thesis is presented by Donald Williams, who argues that it is the example of a sea-fight which misleads us, for it is "craftily chosen to be persuasive because it is peculiarly chancy, mixed up with human volition, and subject to malicious interference and concealment. (Reference to an eclipse tomorrow would not find us half so receptive of the suggestion of its unreality.)"[32] Thus Williams is suggesting that while the present state of affairs might seem to be indeterminate with regard to whether a sea-fight will or will not take place tomorrow, the present state of affairs is clearly not indeterminate with regard to whether an eclipse will or will not take place tomorrow. Aristotle's example is what leads him erroneously to his fatalistic conclusions.

But Williams here misunderstands Aristotle's view, for that view does not imply that the law of excluded middle does not apply to a statement asserting the occurrence of a future eclipse. Indeed, a statement asserting the occurrence of a future eclipse is just the sort of statement to which the law of excluded middle applies; Aristotle believed that it was not up to anyone whether or not a future eclipse would occur. No one can bring about or prevent an eclipse. It is only a contingent event, an event within someone's power to bring about and within someone's power to prevent, which demands a limitation on the law of excluded middle, and a future eclipse is not such a contingent event.

But this sort of reply has led Elizabeth Anscombe to ask

31. Danto, p. 187.
32. Williams, p. 290.

(through one of the participants in a dialogue) "Could anything that can happen make it untrue that the sun rises tomorrow?" And she suggests that there is something that can make it untrue that the sun rises tomorrow, namely "If we continued in darkness, the appearance of the night being continued for the rest of our lives."[33] But nothing whatever can render it untrue that the sun rose yesterday, and so the past is, therefore, fundamentally different from the future, since all past events are necessary, while all future events are contingent. Nothing that anyone has it within his power to do could make it false that an eclipse occurred yesterday, while something that someone has it within his power to do could render it false that an eclipse will occur tomorrow. Thus, although it is correct to assert, concerning all past events, that no one possesses any control over their occurrence, it is not correct to assert, concerning any future events, that no one possesses any control over their occurrence. Whereas the necessity of past events is binding upon us, the so-called "necessity" of future events is simply misleading, for there is always a possibility that someone might do something to prevent a future event.

But is the future in this respect really different from the past? Admittedly, if it is true that there was an eclipse yesterday, nothing that anyone has it within his power to do can render it false that there was an eclipse yesterday. But similarly, if it is true that there will be an eclipse tomorrow, nothing that anyone has it within his power to do can render it false that there will be an eclipse tomorrow. Admittedly, something someone might logically be able to do would render it false that an eclipse will occur tomorrow, e.g. dying in the destruction of the universe today or simply observing the nonoccurrence of an eclipse tomorrow; but similarly, something someone might logically be able to do would render it false that an eclipse occurred yesterday, e.g. view-

33. G. E. M. Anscombe, "Aristotle and the Sea Battle," *Mind*, 65 (1956), 12.

ing our moon in another galaxy today[34] or simply reading in a reliable newspaper that no eclipse occurred yesterday. Indeed, any action which is logically or physically incompatible with the occurrence of an eclipse yesterday or the occurrence of an eclipse tomorrow would render it false that the former occurred or false that the latter occurred. However, given that both eclipses do occur, no one, in fact, has it within his power to perform any such actions. As A. J. Ayer has pointed out:

> What is so is so whenever it occurs, and if it is so, nothing that actually happens can make it not be so. This is not to deny that something *could* make it not be so, in the sense that it is possible to imagine events or situations which are inconsistent with its being so; but again this applies *whenever* it occurs.[35]

Thus, there seems to be no fundamental difference in this respect between the past and the future. If it is true that an eclipse occurred, no one has it within his power to prevent the occurrence of an eclipse, though it is logically possible that someone could do something to prevent its occurrence. Similarly, if it is true that an eclipse will occur, no one has it within his power to prevent the occurrence of an eclipse, though it is logically possible that someone could do something to prevent its occurrence. Thus, Miss Anscombe has given us no good reason for believing either that all future events are contingent (and in this way differ from all past events) or that if it is true that an event *e* will occur, it is still possible that *e* will not occur (in some special sense of "possible" such that if it is true that an event *e* did occur, it is not possible that *e* did not occur).

---

34. This example assumes that the moon cannot go faster than the speed of light and, therefore, could not be in another galaxy today if it took part in an eclipse of our sun yesterday.

35. Ayer, "Fatalism," p. 245.

Before temporarily leaving the discussion of Aristotle's views, I should like to answer some "strange questions" which, according to Rogers Albritton, cast considerable doubt on Aristotle's thesis.[36] Albritton suggests three such questions which he believes are reasonable to ask of Aristotle, assuming his thesis to be true, but which, according to Albritton, call forth absurd replies, and, therefore, cast real doubt on the validity of Aristotle's thesis. They are: "Was it true yesterday that I would now be awake?" "Will it be false tomorrow that I will sneeze next week?" Was it "not yet false in 1920 that she would bear a son in 1938"?[37] Despite Albritton's remarks, which treat these questions and all possible replies to them as absurd, the questions are not at all absurd. The first two are quite straightforward, while the third is ambiguous in a way that suggests it implies a contradiction. I am going to examine and reply to each of these questions in turn and in that way illustrate the import of Aristotle's view of future contingencies.

"Was it true yesterday that I would now be awake?" The answer to this question depends on whether it was the case yesterday that it was contingent that I would be awake now. It was contingent that I would be awake now if it was not necessary that I should be awake now and if it was not impossible that I should be awake now. It was neither necessary nor impossible if it was within someone's power to bring about my being awake now and if it was within someone's power to prevent my being awake now. In the ordinary case I would assume that it is up to a person himself whether he wishes to go to sleep at a certain time, i.e. it is within a person's power to go to sleep and it is within his power not

36. Rogers Albritton, "Present Truth and Future Contingency," *The Philosophical Review, 66* (1957), 32.

37. This third question appears in Albritton's paper as a statement of the form "It was not yet false in 1920 that she would bear a son in 1938." I have reformulated it into a question for the sake of simplicity.

to go to sleep. Assuming that Albritton is discussing an ordinary case (drugs, hypnosis, and excessive periods without sleep aside), the answer to his question is that it was not true yesterday that I would now be awake and it was not false yesterday that I would now be awake. It was, in fact, contingent and, therefore, neither true nor false that I would now be awake.

"Will it be false tomorrow that I will sneeze next week?" The answer to this question depends on whether it will be the case tomorrow that it is contingent that I will sneeze next week. It will be contingent that I will sneeze next week if it will not be necessary tomorrow that I will sneeze next week and it will not be impossible tomorrow that I will sneeze next week. It will be neither necessary nor impossible if it will be within someone's power tomorrow to bring about my sneezing next week and if it will be within someone's power tomorrow to prevent my sneezing next week. In the ordinary case it will be within someone's power tomorrow to bring about my sneezing next week, for he will be able, for example, to give me snuff, thereby forcing me to sneeze. It also will be within someone's power tomorrow to prevent my sneezing next week, for he will be able, for example, to kill me before next week. Assuming that Albritton is discussing an ordinary case, the answer to his question is that it will not be true tomorrow that I will sneeze next week and it will not be false tomorrow that I will sneeze next week. It will be, in fact, contingent and, therefore, neither true nor false that I will sneeze next week.

Was it "not yet the case in 1920 that she would bear a son in 1938"? This question is ambiguous because it is not clear whether she actually bore a son in 1938. Assuming that she did not, we may use the same reasoning that has been used in replies to the first two questions and assert that in ordinary circumstances it was not false in 1920 that she would bear a son in 1938 and it was not true in 1920 that she would bear a son in 1938, for in 1920 it was neither necessary nor impossible that she would bear a son in 1938.

Assuming, on the other hand, that she did bear a son in 1938, it is misleading to speak of it not being false *yet* that she would bear a son in 1938, since, in fact, it is never false that she bears a son in 1938. Again assuming ordinary circumstances to hold, it is not false that she will bear a son in 1938 and it is not *yet* true that she will bear a son in 1938, the reasoning being the same as above. Thus, Albritton's questions which seem to be so phrased as to create confusion are, in fact, answerable without any difficulty—if Aristotle's thesis concerning future contingencies is correctly understood and taken seriously.

It is now time to turn to another philosopher whose views are far less well known than those of Aristotle. This is the Megarian philosopher, Diodorus Cronus. Though his position is somewhat similar to that of Aristotle, they differ in at least one important respect. Aristotle was concerned to avoid fatalisic conclusions and he was led, therefore, in the light of his own arguments to modify the law of excluded middle. Diodorus, on the other hand, from all the historical accounts which we have, seems to have believed in fatalism and sought logically to prove it to be true.

4 The "Master Argument" of Diodorus Cronus

Diodorus Cronus, a young contemporary of Aristotle, was a philosopher of the Megaric school who had a considerable influence on the later Stoic movement. He achieved wide fame as a logician and formulator of philosophical paradoxes. It is one of these paradoxes, the so-called "Master Argument," upon which his fame chiefly rests, and it is this paradox, designed to prove the truth of fatalism, which we shall now consider.

Unfortunately, no writings of Diodorus are extant, and we are forced to piece together the paradox from secondary sources. This is particularly difficult, since although we know the premises of Diodorus' argument and the conclusion he drew, the arguments he used to draw this conclusion are not known. Some commentators are inclined to dismiss Diodorus' arguments, whatever they may be, as simply erroneous, since the unusual conclusion to which they are supposed to lead is considered implausible. It is well to note, however, that although Diodorus' contemporaries, Cleanthes and Chrysippus, both of whom were outstanding logicians, disagreed with Diodorus' conclusion, they chose to deny one of his premises rather than to question his proof. In what follows I will first formulate the paradox as Diodorus appears to have conceived it, and then I will discuss several possible lines of argument which he might have employed to reach his conclusion.[1]

1. In considering arguments which Diodorous might have utilized to prove fatalism, I am not primarily interested in determining

The Master Argument consists essentially of two premises and a conclusion. Premise (1) is "Everything that is past and true is necessary." Premise (2) is "The impossible does not follow from the possible." The conclusion is that "The possible is that which either is or will be."[2] If the conclusion is true, then the only events which anyone has it within his power to bring about are those events which do, in fact, occur, and this amounts to a denial of man's free will. But how can Diodorus logically proceed from premises (1) and (2) to his fatalistic conclusion? Therein lies the puzzle of the Master Argument.

Frederick Copleston has reconstructed the Master Argument in the following way:

(1) "The possible cannot become the impossible."
(2) If "of two contradictories, one has actually come to pass, the other is impossible."
(3) But, "if it had been possible before, the impossible would have come out of the possible."
(4) "Therefore, it was not possible before."
(5) Thus, "only the actual is possible."[3]

Step (1) is equivalent to Diodorus' premise (2). Step (2) is a special case of premise (1). These steps immediately raise the question of what is meant here by the terms "possible" and "impossible." The argument seems to rest on notions of "possible" and "impossible" which are very closely akin to what Aristotle had in mind by the same terms, i.e. an event e is possible if it is not the case that the nonoccurrence of e is necessary, and e is impossible if the nonoccur-

---

whether or not these arguments were actually utilized by Diodorus. What I am interested in determining is the validity of the arguments themselves.

2. Epictetus, *Dissertationes ab Arriano Digestae*, ed. H Schenkl (Leipzig, 1898), II, 19, 1, quoted in Kneale and Kneale, p. 119.

3. Frederick Copleston, *A History of Philosophy* (Garden City, New York, 1962), *1*, 138.

rence of *e* is necessary, *e* being necessary if it is not within anyone's power to prevent its occurrence. Step (2) then seems uncontroversial, since it asserts that if it is true that an event *e* occurred, the nonoccurrence of *e* is impossible, i.e. no one can prevent the occurrence of *e,* and this is surely so.

Step (3) constitutes a *reductio ad absurdum,* for if steps (1) and (2) are acceptable, step (3) follows immediately, given a certain sense of the expression "the impossible would have come out of the possible," viz. the sense that an event which was at one time possible became impossible. This is not to say that a possible event caused an impossible event. Rather, a possibility which existed at one time simply disappeared, i.e. a man's power to prevent the occurrence of an event was lost, thereby turning a possible event into an impossible one. Steps (4) and (5) complete the proof in unexceptionable form.

The reasoning employed in this proof seems to be correct. One is inclined to deny step (1), however, on the ground that, given Diodorus' notions of possibility and impossibility, it does seem reasonable to assert that the impossible *can* follow from the possible, and that no absurdity is involved in holding such a view. In other words, one avoids Diodorus' fatalistic conclusion by asserting that an event which is at one time possible can become impossible. For example, although I had it within my power the day before yesterday to go swimming yesterday, if I did not go swimming yesterday, then it is today no longer within my power to go swimming yesterday. The lapse of time itself thus affects my ability to perform certain actions. Though this view has on occasion been denied, it does not seem to be an implausible assumption, and to admit it does not seem too great a price to pay to avoid fatalism.[4] Thus, although Copleston's reconstruction of Diodorus' Master Argument is consistent and

4. For a full discussion of this point and the implications for the philosophy of time, see Chapter 8.

proves what it is intended to prove, it fails to make a strong enough case for fatalism, since the denial of one of its assumptions seems reasonable and appears to involve one in no special difficulties.

Another reconstruction of Diodorus' Master Argument has been attempted by Jaakko Hintikka. In order to understand his reconstruction, one must first understand his use of the notion of "possibility":

> In order to examine whether a premiss of the form "it is possible that p" is compatible with a number of other premisses, we may assume p. If we can deduce from p a consequence (say r) such that "it is impossible that r" follows from the other premisses, then our set of premisses is inconsistent. If this never happens, then "it is possible that p cannot cause an inconsistency in our set of premisses. The possible thus is, in a sense, exactly "that which, being assumed, results in nothing impossible."[5]

Keeping this notion of "possibility" in mind, let us consider Hintikka's reconstruction:

(1) "Any true statement concerning the past is necessary."[6]

(2) "If a possibility is assumed to be realized, no impossible conclusions follow."

(3) Assume that, concerning some event symbolized by p, "it is not the case that p nor will it be the case at any later moment of time."

(4) Assume that it is possible that p.

(5) Given (2) and (4) one may assume that "at time t_0 it will be true that p." Let us make that assumption.

5. Jaakko Hintikka, "Aristotle and the 'Master Argument' of Diodorus," *American Philosophical Quarterly, 1* (1964), 104.

6. "Necessary" here clearly means "irrefutable," i.e. no man can falsify it.

(6) "Consider any moment of time t_1 later than t_0, say the day after t_0 . . . at time t_1 it will be true that p was the case yesterday."

(7) From (3) it follows that "at time t_0 it will be false that p."

(8) Thus, "at time t_1 it will be false that p was the case yesterday."

(9) Given (1) and (8) it follows that "at time t_1 it will be true that it is impossible for p to have been the case yesterday."[7]

Hintikka notes that (5) and (7) are not sufficient to produce the impossibility which Diodorus is attempting to show, since although it is not the case that both (5) and (7) can be true, it does not follow from this that one of the two statements is impossible, but only that one of them is false. To achieve the desired impossibility Diodorus must complete the proof as he has done.

Hintikka's proof is logically sound: the premises do logically imply the conclusion.[8] Furthermore, Hintikka's proof does parallel Diodorus' Master Argument. Step (1) is equivalent to Diodorus' premise (1). Step (2) is equivalent to Diodorus' premise (2). The conclusion of Hintikka's proof is equivalent to Diodorus' conclusion: the only possible events are those which do, in fact, occur.

Nevertheless, Hintikka's reconstruction of Diodorus' Master Argument does not seem satisfactory. The doubtful step in Hintikka's proof is step (2). This step is an interpreta-

7. Ibid , pp. 106–07. Hintikka's reconstruction (which I have formalized more succinctly than he does) is a more subtle version of a previous attempt made by Eduard Zeller. See "Über den κυριεύων des Megarikers Diodorus," in *Kleine Schriften,* ed. O. H. Leuze (Berlin, 1910), *1,* 252–62. Zeller's work is discussed at some length in Hintikka's article.

8. I am not reviewing the proof step by step, since the logic seems unexceptionable.

tion of Diodorus' premise (2), the same premise whose interpretation constituted a weak link in Copleston's proof, since the premise as interpreted by Copleston could be denied without too great an inconvenience. Hintikka's interpretation of this premise seems even weaker than Copleston's, for one can deny it while denying, as one could not deny in the case of Copleston's proof, that the lapse of time itself affects a man's abilities.

Why should a possibility be realizable without incurring an impossibility? If it is possible that a sea-fight will take place tomorrow and it is also possible that a sea-fight will not take place tomorrow, that surely does not imply that both possibilities can be realized without incurring an impossibility. What it does imply is that if one possibility is realized and the other is not, no impossibility will follow, and, likewise, if the second possibility is realized and the first is not, no impossibility will follow.

To bring out this point more clearly consider an example presented by Diodorus' opponent, Chrysippus.[9] He claimed that it is possible for a certain jewel to be broken at a specific time (call that time t_0) even if it is not broken at that time. Surely Chrysippus did not mean to assert that if we assume that the jewel is not broken at t_0, then we can also assume that it is broken at t_0 without incurring an impossibility. Clearly what Chrysippus meant to assert was that although the jewel is not broken at t_0, under certain possible circumstances which will not, in fact, occur the jewel would be broken at t_0. It is no argument against Chrysippus to point out that if the jewel is not broken at t_0, then at some future time (call that time t_1) it is impossible for the jewel to have been broken at t_0. Chrysippus was not claiming that at t_1 it is possible for the jewel to be broken at t_0. What he claimed was that at some time prior to t_0 there were possible circumstances which, had they occurred, would have re-

9. Cicero, p. 207.

sulted in the jewel's breaking at t_0. It is simply irrelevant to point out that it is impossible for these circumstances to have obtained once t_0 has passed.

Thus it is simply not clear why anyone should be committed to Hintikka's interpretation of premise (2), or what important philosophical principle is being relinquished if one denies Hintikka's interpretation of this premise. Thus, Hintikka's proof, though it is logically sound, is not a satisfactory proof of fatalism, for one of its premises is open to serious doubt.

A more persuasive reconstruction of the Master Argument has been offered by Arthur Prior.[10] He puts the two premises of Diodorus in the following way: (1) "whatever has been the case cannot now not have been the case, and (2) "whatever definitely implies an impossibility is itself impossible." Prior then supplies two other premises which he believes Diodorus and his contemporaries to have accepted. Premise (3) is that "anything's being the case definitely implies that it has not been the case that it will never be the case." Premise (4) is that "if anything now neither is nor will be the case, then it has by now been the case that it will never be the case." Let us first examine these four premises. Premise (1) is a restatement of Diodorus' premise that "Everything that is past and true is necessary." Prior interprets "necessary" as referring to propositions, a necessary proposition being one which no man can falsify. Thus, a true proposition asserting that a certain event occurred is necessary, since it cannot be falsified by any man. Martha Kneale has objected to this reconstruction of Diodorus' first premise, for she claims that whereas "what is true about the past

10 Prior discusses the Master Argument in *Time and Modality* (Oxford, 1957), pp. 84–103; "Diodoran Modalities," *The Philosophical Quarterly, 5* (1955), 205–13; "Diodorus and Modal Logic," *The Philosophical Quarterly, 8* (1958), 226–30; "Tense-Logic and the Continuity of Time," *Studia Logica, 13* (1962), 133–51.

remains so and cannot be altered," a statement[11] such as the one Prior uses is supposedly about the past. "It has been the case that it will never be seen" is not really a statement about the past, for the statement can also be expressed without loss of meaning in a sentence whose main verb is in the future tense: "It will always be the case that it will never be seen."[12] Mrs. Kneale is thus arguing that not every statement in the past tense is a statement about the past, and it is only a statement about the past of which necessity can properly be predicted on the ground that the past is unalterable.

But surely, to say that it will always be true that an event *e* will never occur is not to say that it has always been true that *e* will never occur, for it may not be true that it *was* true that *e* would never occur, though it *is* true that *e* will never occur. For instance, if it was true last year that I would go swimming today, then if anyone had asserted last year that I would go swimming today, he would have spoken truly. That is certainly a fact about the past. Thus, if it had been up to me yesterday whether I would go swimming today, it would have been within my power yesterday to alter the past, for it would have been within my power yesterday to make it false last year that if anyone had asserted last year that I would go swimming today, he would have spoken truly. It may be true today that I go swimming, and in that case it would be true next year that I went swimming today, but this implies neither that it was true last year that I would go swimming today nor that it was not up to me yesterday whether I would go swimming today. Thus, contrary to what Mrs. Kneale would have us believe, what is true at a past time is a fact about the past as well as a fact about what is true.[13]

11. "Proposition" and "statement" are used here synonymously. A "sentence" is an expression of a proposition or statement.

12. Kneale and Kneale, p. 121.

13. For a further discussion of this point, see Chapter 5.

Premise (2) is a restatement of Diodorus' premise that "The impossible does not follow from the possible." Here Prior interprets "follow" as meaning "logically implies." Thus, the reference is again to the possibility and impossibility of propositions. A proposition is impossible if its denial is necessary, and a proposition is possible if it is not the case that its denial is necessary. Thus, Prior's second premise is asserting that if a proposition is such that its denial can be falsified by some person, then that proposition cannot logically imply another proposition which is such that its denial cannot be falsified by some person. Here for the first time we find a plausible interpretation of Diodorus' premise (2): if a proposition P is such that $\sim P$ can be falsified by some person, and a proposition Q is such that $\sim Q$ cannot be falsified by some person, then P cannot imply Q. If P could imply Q, then $\sim Q$ could imply $\sim P$ (by *modus tollens*), and a necessary proposition could imply a nonnecessary proposition, which is not the case.

Prior's premise (3) simply states that if something is the case, e.g. a sea-fight today, then at no time was it true that there would not be a sea-fight today. This seems undeniable, for if at some time it was true that there would not be a sea-fight today, then it would seem to follow that there is no sea-fight today. But, by hypothesis, there is a sea-fight today. Thus, premise (3) seems unexceptionable.

Prior's premise (4) states that if it is not true now that there will be a sea-fight next week, and if it will never be true that there will be a sea-fight next week, then it was true that there would not be a sea-fight next week. The denial of this premise is equivalent to a denial of the law of excluded middle, for if it was not true that there would not be a sea-fight next week, it certainly was not false that there would not be a sea-fight next week (for, in fact, there will not be a sea-fight next week). Thus, Prior's four premises seem to be acceptable. Now what of the proof itself?

Prior's proof is as follows:

(1) Assume that "there is a shell at the bottom of some shallow water which neither is nor ever will be seen."

(2) "Since it neither is nor ever will be seen, it has been the case that it will never be seen."

(3) Hence, by premise (1) "it cannot now not have been the case that it will never be seen," i.e. "it is now *impossible* for it not to have been the case that it will never be seen."

(4) By premise (2) anything which implies an impossibility is itself impossible and "the supposition that the shell is being seen *would* imply that it has not been the case that the shell will never be seen; this supposition is therefore an impossible one."[14]

Generalizing this conclusion, it appears that for any case in which a supposed possibility is never realized it follows that there never was such a possibility, and thus the events which occur are the only events which can possibly occur, and this is fatalism, the doctrine which Diodorus sought to prove.

Step (1) is an unexceptionable premise. Step (2) is a simple application of premise (4) to step (1). Thus, if there is a shell at the bottom of some shallow water which neither is nor ever will be seen, it has been the case that it will never be seen, since according to premise (4) if anything now neither is nor will be the case, then it has by now been the case that it will never be the case. Step (3) applies premise (1) to step (2). Thus, since it has been the case that the shell will never be seen, it follows that it is now impossible for it now not to have been the case that it will never be seen, for according to premise (1), whatever has been the case cannot now not have been the case, i.e. the past is in at least one important sense unalterable. Step (4) is an application of premise (2) to step (3). Thus, if it is now

14. Prior, *Time and Modality,* pp. 86–87.

impossible for it not to have been the case that the shell
will never be seen, the assumption that the shell is seen is
also impossible, for this assumption implies that it was the
case that the shell would be seen, which is impossible, and
by premise (2) only an impossible proposition can imply an
impossible proposition. Thus, Prior's proof seems to be
sound.

Jaakko Hintikka, in discussing Prior's reconstruction of
the Master Argument, states that

> Prior's interpretation is entirely based on the assump-
> tion that Diodorus would have taken a statement con-
> cerning the truth of past predictions as being a state-
> ment concerning the past in the sense of Diodorus'
> first premise . . . I find this assumption rather strange,
> and I fail to perceive anything in the texts that un-
> ambiguously supports it.[15]

This objection appears to be entirely a historical one, since
it challenges the assumption that Diodorus would have made
use of a certain type of argument. But as this objection
leaves entirely untouched the validity of the argument itself,
and since it is the validity of the argument which is under
consideration, this type of objection need not concern us
here.

Martha Kneale has presented another objection to Prior's
reconstruction. She argues that Diodorus' argument as Prior
understands it leads to the conclusion that "the modal words
'possible' and 'necessary' . . . [are] superfluous."[16] Since
it is quite obvious that these words are not superfluous, any
argument which implies that these words are superfluous
must be erroneous.

The objection Mrs. Kneale presents here is especially
important because it is so often raised against proponents

15. Hintikka, p. 101.
16. Kneale and Kneale, p. 117.

of fatalistic arguments. She argues that these arguments collapse the usual modal notions of possible and necessary into one, that all true statements become necessary, and all false statements become impossible.

While this sort of objection may seem to carry great weight, the very results implied by fatalistic arguments are precisely what these arguments are intended to imply; these are necessary conditions of a fatalistic view. If fatalism is true, then there are no possible events which are not necessary. This is not to assert that there is no distinction between a possible event and a necessary event, but rather to point out that although there *is* a distinction between these two kinds of events, the first class of events, the class of all simply possible events, is empty (i.e. there are no possible events which are not necessary). To take a simple example of this sort of argument, if I assert that all living beings are mortal, this is not to obliterate the distinction between mortal and immortal living beings. It is just this distinction which is being utilized in the assertion that there are no living beings who are immortal. Similarly, though there is an important distinction between possible and necessary events, there are (on the fatalistic view) no events which are possible but not necessary.[17]

A fatalist is also committed to the view that all true statements are necessary and all false statements are impossible, i.e. no person can falsify a true statement and no person can render true a false statement. This may be a strange position, but it is precisely the fatalistic viewpoint, and it is no argu-

17. Fatalism is thus not subject to the charge that it obliterates certain contrasting notions, e.g. the distinction between (1) events within my power to bring about and to prevent, and (2) events not within my power to bring about and to prevent. Fatalism does not deny the distinction between (1) and (2). It simply asserts that class (1) is empty. This is the same strategy commonly employed in distinguishing unicorns and nonunicorns and then asserting that there are no unicorns.

ment against this viewpoint to note that the fatalist is committed to it.

Thus, Mrs. Kneale's objection essentially points out that
the acceptance of a fatalistic position commits one to certain
strange opinions. But this is not to refute fatalism, since it
is precisely these strange views which a fatalist accepts and
which a fatalistic argument, such as that of Diodorus, seeks
to prove.

One could avoid Diodorus' fatalistic conclusion by denying premise (4): "if anything now neither is nor will be the
case, then it has by now been the case that it will never be
the case." To deny this would be, as we have seen, to deny
that every proposition must be either true, or if not true,
then false. To relinquish the law of excluded middle may
not be too great a price to pay to avoid fatalism, and, indeed,
it was just such a move which Aristotle made to avoid the
fatalistic conclusions of his own arguments. But Prior has
suggested that this is but one way in which one can avoid
the conclusion of Diodorus' argument. Prior himself suggests
that perhaps the most convenient way to avoid Diodorus'
conclusion is to maintain that

> where the question as to whether p will eventuate or
> not is undecided, we might say that both "It will be the
> case that p" and "It will be the case that not p" are
> plain false, while "It will not be the case that p" . . .
> and "It will not be the case that not p" are both plain
> true.[18]

This same sort of strategy has been supported somewhat
differently by Charles Hartshorne, who writes:

> Any will, will-not, or may-or-may-not statement, if not
> true, is definitely false; it can only be right or wrong to
> say that all, or that only some, or that no possibilities
> at a specified present or past time for a later time

18. Prior, *Time and Modality*, pp. 95–96.

include A. But whichever of the three statements is true, the others are both false . . . The third "value" is thus in the statement forms, not in their truth status.[19]

Thus, both Prior and Hartshorne are suggesting that one need not suspend the law of excluded middle in order to avoid reaching fatalistic conclusions.[20]

Let us first turn to Hartshorne's views. According to Hartshorne, if, for instance, it is up to me whether a sea-fight will take place tomorrow, then it is false that a sea-fight will take place tomorrow, and it is false that a sea-fight will not take place tomorrow. The whole truth is expressed by asserting that a sea-fight may or may not take place tomorrow. This position thus seems to avoid the brunt of Diodorus' argument by denying premise (3), for if it is false now that there will be a sea-fight tomorrow, and if it is false now that there will not be a sea-fight tomorrow, then assuming that tomorrow there is a sea-fight, it is not the case tomorrow that "anything's being the case definitely implies that it has not been the case that it will never be the case." Hartshorne has thus denied premise (3) without suspending the law of excluded middle and without, according to him, giving up any other important logical principle.

But has not Hartshorne actually preserved the law of excluded middle only at the cost of the law of contradiction? Let us take a specific example. Assume once again that it is now up to me whether a sea-fight takes place at a certain time tomorrow. In other words it is within my power to bring about the sea-fight, and it is also within my power

19. Hartshorne, p. 47.

20. A position similar to that of Prior and Hartshorne has been defended by Arthur Danto, *Analytic Philosophy of History*, Chap. 9. Danto, however, argues that *all* statements about the future are false, whereas Prior and Hartshorne seem to agree with Aristotle that the future is "fixed" with regard to certain events, though not with regard to all events Danto denies this. Nevertheless, the logical structure of his position is identical to that of Prior and Hartshorne.

to prevent the sea-fight. Aristotle and Hartshorne would both seem to agree that it is not true now that the sea-fight will take place tomorrow, and it is likewise not true now that the sea-fight will not take place tomorrow. Aristotle, however, would affirm that it is *not* false that a sea-fight will take place tomorrow, whereas Hartshorne would affirm that it *is* false that a sea-fight will take place tomorrow. Aristotle admits that he has relinquished the law of excluded middle, i.e. he has given up the principle that every proposition must be true, or if not true, then false. He *has* clearly given up this principle, for if it is not true that a sea-fight will take place tomorrow, and it is not false that a sea-fight will take place tomorrow, then it plainly follows that there is a proposition which is not true and not false, viz. the proposition affirming that there will be a sea-fight tomorrow. Indeed, there is at least one more proposition which is not true and not false, viz. the proposition affirming that there will not be a sea-fight tomorrow.

Now what of Hartshorne's position? He affirms that it is false that there will be a sea-fight tomorrow and it is also false that there will not be a sea-fight tomorrow. He clearly has not rejected the law of excluded middle, for he has not suggested that any proposition is not true and not false. The proposition that there will be a sea-fight tomorrow is, according to him, false; the proposition that there will not be a sea-fight tomorrow, is, according to him, false; the proposition that there may be a sea-fight tomorrow is true, as is the proposition that there may not be a sea-fight tomorrow. None of these is not true and not false.

But what of the law of contradiction? The law of contradiction affirms that in the case of any proposition, if that proposition is true, then its contradictory must be false, whereas if the proposition in question is false, then its contradictory must be true. The contradictory of a proposition is the denial of that proposition. Thus, the contradictory of "there is (was, will be) a sea-fight at place P and time T"

is "there is not (was not, will not be) a sea-fight at place P and time T." Similarly, the latter is the contradictory of the former. In general, p and $\sim p$ are contradictories of each other, as are $\sim p$ and $\sim \sim p$ for any interpretation of p and for any tense in which p is expressed. Note that the law of contradiction as I have presented it is not equivalent to the law of excluded middle. For example, it would be no exception to the law of contradiction to find a proposition which was neither true nor false, though to find such a proposition would be an exception to the law of excluded middle. For example, if it is neither true nor false that a sea-fight will take place tomorrow, that is perfectly compatible with the assertion that if a statement is true, its contradictory must be false, and vice versa. It is not compatible, however, with the statement that every proposition must be either true, or if not true, then false.

Now, Hartshorne asserts that it is false that a sea-fight will take place tomorrow and it is false that a sea-fight will not take place tomorrow. If we represent the proposition "a sea-fight will take place tomorrow" by p, then Hartshorne seems to be affirming that p is false and $\sim p$ is false. But this is surely to deny the law of contradiction, for p and $\sim p$ are certainly contradictories, and as such, one must be true and the other false.

Here Hartshorne affirms that, in the case of a statement affirming or denying the occurrence in the future of a contingent event, it and its denial are not contradictories, but contraries such that both may be false, though not both may be true. At this point it is no longer clear what Hartshorne means by a contradictory or what he means by affirming that one proposition is the contradictory of some other proposition. Since the propositions "there was a sea-fight" and "there was not a sea-fight" are contradictories, so are the propositions "there will be a sea-fight" and "there will not be a sea-fight."

Thus, whereas Aristotle chose to deny the law of excluded middle, Hartshorne chooses to deny the law of contradiction. It is clear that to affirm the doctrine of future contingencies and thereby deny the Master Argument one does so at a certain cost, whether it be relinquishing the law of excluded middle or relinquishing the law of contradiction.

Let us turn next to Prior's views. According to Prior, if it is up to me whether a sea-fight will take place tomorrow, then it is false that it will be the case that a sea-fight will take place tomorrow, and it is also false that it will be the case that a sea-fight will not take place tomorrow. However, it is true that it will not be the case that a sea-fight will take place tomorrow, and it is also true that it will not be the case that a sea-fight will not take place tomorrow. Thus, Prior, like Hartshorne, avoids the fatalistic conclusion of Diodorus' argument by denying premise (3), for if it is now false that it will be the case that a sea-fight will take place tomorrow and it is now true that it will not be the case that a sea-fight will take place tomorrow, then assuming that tomorrow there is a sea-fight, it is not the case tomorrow that "anything's being the case definitely implies that it has not been the case that it will never be the case." Thus, Prior has denied premise (3) without suspending the law of excluded middle and without, according to him, giving up any other important logical principle.

But has not Prior, just as Hartshorne, actually preserved the law of excluded middle only at the cost of the law of contradiction?

He has not denied the law of excluded middle, for although he affirms that it is false that it will be the case that a sea-fight will take place tomorrow, he also affirms that it is true that it will not be the case that a sea-fight will take place tomorrow. Similarly, although he affirms that it is false that it will be the case that a sea-fight will not take place tomorrow, he also affirms that it is true that it will not be the case that a sea-fight will not take place tomorrow. Thus, Prior has not suggested, as Aristotle did, that there is a

proposition which is neither true nor false, and, consequently, he has not denied the law of excluded middle.

But what of the law of contradiction? If, as Prior asserts,
it is false that it will be the case that a sea-fight will take
place tomorrow, and it is true that it will not be the case
that a sea-fight will take place tomorrow, it follows that
there will not be a sea-fight tomorrow. If, as Prior also
asserts, it is false that it will be the case that a sea-fight will
not take place tomorrow, and it is true that it will not be
the case that a sea-fight will not take place tomorrow, then
it follows that there will be a sea-fight tomorrow, and this
is in direct contradiction to the previous conclusion that
there will not be a sea-fight tomorrow.

To such an argument Prior replies that although it is
false that it will be the case that a sea-fight will not take
place tomorrow, and it is true that it will not be the case
that a sea-fight will not take place tomorrow, it does not
follow that there will be a sea-fight tomorrow. But, if it
will not be the case that a sea-fight will not take place
tomorrow, then it will be the case that a sea-fight will take
place tomorrow, and this is in direct contradiction to Prior's
view that it is false that it will be the case that a sea-fight will
take place tomorrow. In answer to this point Prior argues
that from the fact that it will not be the case that a sea-fight
will not take place tomorrow, it does not follow that it will
be the case that a sea-fight will take place tomorrow. But, if
we represent the proposition "a sea-fight will take place
tomorrow" by p, it seems totally arbitrary to assert that "it
will not be the case that $\sim p$" does not imply that "it will be
the case that p." Why could not one with equal validity claim
that "it is not the case that $\sim p$" does not imply that "it is
the case that p"? And this claim clearly involves the rejec-
tion of the law of excluded middle, which is precisely what
Prior was attempting to avoid.

What is again clear is that if one wishes to affirm Aristotle's doctrine of future contingencies and thereby deny

Diodorus' Master Argument, one must relinquish either
the law of excluded middle or the law of contradiction.[21]

In Chapter 6 we shall discuss a modern argument for
fatalism, one which differs somewhat both from that presented by Aristotle and from that presented by Diodorus
Cronus. However, before turning to that modern argument,
we will examine the problem of fatalism as it appears in
the attempts of many thinkers, especially in the medieval
period, to dissolve the apparent logical incompatibility
between a belief in God's omniscience and a belief in man's
free will.

21. Why it seems preferable to relinquish the law of excluded
middle will become clear in Chapter 7. The need to relinquish this
law is defended by Nicholas Rescher in his recent article, "A Version
of the 'Master Argument' of Diodorus," *The Journal of Philosophy,
63* (1966), 438–45. Rescher's reconstruction of the argument which
is done in purely logical notation seems to me correct. It is similar
to Prior's reconstruction, though it contains certain technical im-
provements.

5 Theological Fatalism

Many thinkers have discussed the problem of fatalism within the context of what may appear at first to be a purely theological issue: does the assumption of God's omniscience logically commit one to deny man's free will? The answer to this question has implications which extend beyond the area of theology. Indeed, it is my contention that at least one proof which demonstrates that God's omniscience is logically incompatible with man's free will can be utilized with slight alterations to show that fatalism is true. The issue of fatalism, however, has received much less attention than the theological issue of the logical incompatibility of God's omniscience and man's free will. Therefore, I will first discuss this latter issue and then draw the parallels between it and the issue of fatalism.[1]

In what follows I will offer a proof designed to show that the assumption of God's omniscience is logically incompatible with the assumption of man's free will. I will then defend this proof against all the important objections I know. Finally, I will alter the proof slightly, without altering its logical structure, and thereby eliminate all reference to theological issues. What then remains is a strong argument in support of fatalism.

It should be made clear at the outset, however, that the proof which I am going to present is not supposed to show

1. It is not my intention to present a historical survey of discussions of the problem of the logical incompatibility of God's omniscience and man's free will. I will discuss this problem only in so far as it seems to me to cast light on the issue of fatalism.

that God exists, or that God, if He exists, is omniscient. What the proof is supposed to show is that if God exists, and if He is omniscient, then man does not have free will.

Let us first examine the term "omniscient." An omniscient being is one who knows everything which is true.[2] If it is true that an eclipse occurred last year, then an omniscient being knows that an eclipse occurred last year. If it is true that an eclipse is presently occurring, then an omniscient being knows that an eclipse is presently occurring. If it is true that an eclipse will occur next year, then an omniscient being knows that an eclipse will occur next year. It might be argued that no one, including God, is omniscient. This may be so, but it has no bearing on the question under discussion, since it denies the truth of an assumption whose truth is of no concern in this question.

Let us next examine the term "free will." As I explicated this term earlier, to assert that man has free will is to assert that, at least on some occasions, man performs certain free acts—certain acts which he had it within his power to refrain from, but which he, instead, performed.[3]

Now let us proceed to the specific problem. I assume that most people believe that at the moment they are reading this page (call that moment t_2), they are freely continuing to read (call that act R), since they have it within their power to stop reading. The question is this: if God exists and is omniscient, is R a free act? Consider the following proof:[4]

2. An omniscient being does not know that which is false, but does know that certain propositions are false. For example, it is false that I have eleven fingers. An omniscient being does not know that I have eleven fingers, but does know that it is false that I have eleven fingers.

3. See Chapter 1.

4. The following proof is based on a somewhat similar proof presented in Nelson Pike's "Divine Omniscience and Voluntary Action," *The Philosophical Review, 74* (1965), 33–34.

(1) Every proposition must be either true, or if not true, then false.

(2) At t_1 (assume t_1 to be exactly one day earlier than t_2) it is true, or if not true, then false, that I will perform R at t_2.

(3) God knows everything which is true.

(4) Assume that it is true at t_1 that I will perform R at t_2.

(5) Thus, God knows at t_1 that I will perform R at t_2.

(6) But if God knows at t_1 that I will perform R at t_2, then if it is within my power to refrain from performing R at t_2, it would follow that it is within my power to confute God's knowledge, i.e. it is within my power to make it true that God knew what was false, and since what God knows is true, this would imply that I could confute the law of contradiction, which is absurd.

(7) Therefore, it is not within my power to refrain from performing R at t_2.

(8) Assume next that it is false at t_1 that I will perform R at t_2.

(9) Thus, God knows at t_1 that I will not perform R at t_2.

(10) But if God knows at t_1 that I will not perform R at t_2, then if it is within my power to perform R at t_2, it would follow that it is within my power to confute God's knowledge, i.e. it is within my power to make it true that God knew what was false, and since what God knows is true, this would imply that I could confute the law of contradiction, which is absurd.

(11) Therefore, it is not within my power to perform R at t_2.

(12) Thus, whether it is true at t_1 or false at t_1 that I perform R at t_2, R is not a free action.

A similar argument can be presented to show that any human action is not really a free action. Thus, we seem forced to conclude that God's omniscience precludes man's free will and that a belief in one ought logically to preclude a belief in the other.

The type of argument which I have presented above has been attacked on various grounds. Leibniz argued against it in the following way:

> They say that what is foreseen cannot fail to exist and they say so truly; but it follows not that what is foreseen is necessary. For necessary truth is that whereof the contrary is impossible or implies a contradiction. Now the truth which states that I shall write tomorrow is not of that nature, it is not necessary. Yet, supposing that God foresees it, it is necessary that it come to pass, that is, the consequence is necessary, namely that it exist, since it has been foreseen; for God is infallible. This is what is termed a *hypothetical necessity*. But our concern is not this necessity; it is an *absolute* necessity that is required to be able to say that an action is necessary, that it is not contingent, that it is not the effect of free choice.[5]

Leibniz is certainly correct in asserting that no action is logically necessary simply because God knows that it will occur. But, as we have seen, the sort of necessity relevant to man's free will is not logical necessity. The sort of necessity which is relevant to man's free will is this: an event is necessary if no man can prevent its occurrence. If God knows that I will perform a certain action A tomorrow, it does not follow that A is logically necessary. It does follow, however (and this is what my argument was intended to show) that it is not within my power to prevent A, and a man

5. Gottfried Leibniz, *Theodicy, Essays on the Goodness of God, the Freedom of Man and the Origin of Evil*, trans. E. M. Huggard (Edinburgh and London, 1952), pt. I, sec. 37, p. 144.

does not have free will if it is not within his power to prevent any event which does, in fact, occur. Thus, it is possible for no man to have free will even if no event which ever has occurred, is occurring, or will occur is logically necessary.[6]

St. Augustine believed the sort of proof I presented to be fallacious for various reasons. He claimed that "God fore-knows all the things of which He Himself is the Cause, and yet He is not the Cause of all that He foreknows."[7] Now, St. Augustine is certainly correct in asserting that God's knowledge of a certain event's occurrence is not the cause of that event's occurrence. To take the example used in my proof, God's knowledge does not cause me either to perform R or to refrain from R. Indeed, the proof was formulated without any reference to caused actions. It is consistent with the proof to assert that my action was caused by certain unconscious factors, or by the action of another person, or by any one of a number of other possible causes. But this is not to imply that God's foreknowledge has nothing whatever to do with my performing R or refraining from R. His foreknowledge is a sufficient condition for my action,[8] though it is not its cause. That was the point of the proof I presented, and it is irrelevant to this point to note that God is not the cause of that which he foreknows.

Jonathan Edwards made this point very clearly when he argued:

> Whether prescience be the thing that *makes* the event necessary or no, it alters not the case. Infallible fore-

6. It is not my purpose in this chapter to discuss the philosophy of Leibniz or of any other philosopher. I am simply discussing certain standard objections to a specific proof in an effort to determine whether the proof is sound.

7. St. Augustine, *On Free Choice of the Will,* trans. Anna S. Benjamin and L. H. Hackstaff (New York, 1964), Book III, sec. 4, p. 95.

8. For the explication of the term "sufficient condition" see Chapter 3.

72 FATE, LOGIC, AND TIME

knowledge may *prove* the necessity of the event foreknown, and yet not be the thing which *causes* the
necessity. If the foreknowledge be absolute, this *proves*
the event known to be necessary, or proves that 'tis
impossible but that the event should be, by some means
or other.[9]

In other words, if God knows that I will perform R, that
implies no information as to the cause of R. It does imply,
however, or to use Edwards' word, "prove," that I cannot
refrain from R, and it is my ability to refrain from R as well
as to perform it which is crucial to the question of whether
R is a free action and whether I have free will.

St. Augustine also made the following point:

It is not the case . . . that because God foreknew what
would be in the power of our wills, there is for that
reason nothing in the power of our wills. For he who
foreknew this did not foreknow nothing. Moreover,
if He who foreknew what would be in the power of
our wills did not foreknow nothing, but something,
assuredly, even though He did foreknow, there is
something in the power of our wills.[10]

But this surely begs the entire issue. If it is possible that
God foreknows that I will act freely, then it is true that I
will act freely. But the entire point of my proof was to
demonstrate that it is not possible for God to foreknow
that I will act freely. If God knew at t_1 that I would do R
at t_2, then I was not able to refrain from R at t_2 (for reasons
already given). Thus, if God knew at t_1 I would do R at
t_2, it would follow that I did R at t_2, but not freely. It does
not seem to be possible then that God could have known

9. Jonathan Edwards, *Freedom of the Will,* ed. Paul Ramsey
(New Haven, 1957), p. 263.
10. St. Augustine, *The City of God,* trans. Marcus Dods (New
York, 1950), Book V, sec. 10, p. 157.

at t_1 that I would freely do R at t_2. If He did know at t_1 that I would do R at t_2, then R was not a free action; and if God knew at t_1 that I would freely perform R at t_2, then God's knowledge was erroneous—which is a contradiction.

St. Augustine presents another objection along a somewhat different line, which has become a standard "refutation" of arguments designed to show the logical incompatibility of God's omniscience and man's free will. He argues that, "Your recollection of events in the past does not compel them to occur. In the same way God's foreknowledge of future events does not compel them to take place."[11]

Now admittedly, the fact that I remember[12] that an event occurred does not cause (and in that sense "compel") that past event to have occurred. Similarly, if God knows that a future event will occur, He does not thereby cause the future event to occur. But my knowledge of the occurrence of a past event is intimately connected with the occurrence of that event. If I know that an event e occurred, it follows that (1) the event e occurs, (2) e occurs prior to the present moment, and (3) it is not now within my power to prevent the occurrence of e. Of course, I might do something now which is a sufficient condition for the occurrence of e in the past. For example, if I raise my arm, that is sufficient for my having been alive an hour before. I can, however, perform only those actions which are sufficient conditions for events which actually took place, for if I could perform actions which are sufficient conditions for events which did not take place, it would be within my power to alter what happened in the past, and that is not the case.

Similarly, if God knows that an event e will occur, it follows that (1) the event e occurs, (2) e occurs after the present moment, and (3) it is not now within my power to prevent the occurrence of e. Of course, I might now do

11. St. Augustine, *On Free Choice*, Book III, sec. 4, p. 95.
12. I am assuming here that to "remember" an event occurred carries with it the implication that the event did, in fact, occur.

something which is a sufficient condition for the occurrence
of *e* in the future. For example, if I hang my enemy, that
is sufficient for his death a few moments later. I can, however, only perform actions which are sufficient conditions
for events which actually will take place, for if I could
perform actions which are sufficient conditions for events
which will not take place, it would be within my power to
alter what will happen in the future, and there is no reason
to assume that that is the case.

Thus, God's foreknowledge does not compel future events
in any way that my knowledge of past events does not
compel past events. But, my knowledge of past events is a
sufficient condition for the occurrence of those past events,
i.e. from the fact that I know that a certain event *e* occurred,
it follows that *e* is unalterable, that no person has it within
his power to prevent the occurrence of *e*. Similarly, then,
God's foreknowledge is a sufficient condition for the occurrence of those events which He foreknows, i.e. from the
fact that God knows that a certain event *e* will occur, it
follows that *e* is unalterable, that no person has it within
his power to prevent the occurrence of *e*. If "A compels B"
means "A is sufficient for B," then memory does, contrary
to St. Augustine, compel the occurrence of what is remem-
bered, and foreknowledge does, contrary to St. Augustine,
compel the occurrence of what is foreknown.[13]

Another objection to the sort of proof I presented was
suggested by Friedrich Schleiermacher. He argued:

> In the same way we estimate the intimacy of relation-
> ship between two persons by the foreknowledge one
> has of the actions of the other, without supposing that
> in either case the one or the other's freedom has thereby

13 It is interesting to note that the above line of argument constitutes a second proof for the logical incompatibility of God's
omniscience and man's free will, a proof which is logically independent of the formal proof I presented previously.

been endangered. So even divine foreknowledge cannot
endanger freedom.[14]

Schleiermacher is correct in his assertion that God's
knowledge endangers man's free will no more so than does
a man's knowledge. But, as a matter of fact, either one of
them is sufficient to deny free will. However—and this is
the misleading point in Schleiermacher's argument—men
do not, in fact, have knowledge of the future as God, by
hypothesis, does. God being omniscient knows everything
which is true about the future. A man, on the other hand,
can be said to know very few things, if any, about the
future. It is said that every man knows that he will die. This
is as clear a case as any of a man's knowing a future fact.
What does this knowledge entail? Surely, if a man knows
that he will die, that entails that it is not within his power
to remain alive forever. Thus, a man's knowing that a future
event will occur entails that he cannot prevent the occurrence of that event. If a man knew not only that he was
going to die but also when, where, and how he was going
to die, that would entail that it was not within his power to
avoid death at the known time, at the known place, and in
the known manner. Of course, normally when we speak of
a man's knowledge that I will perform a certain action, we
mean that a man has good evidence that I will perform that
action, though there is, in fact, a chance that he might be
wrong. Common parlance always allows a certain proba-
bility that a man who "knows" something about the future
might not be correct. It is just this leeway for error which
is usually eliminated in speaking of a man's knowing that
he will die, and it is this same leeway for error which is
eliminated in speaking of God's foreknowledge, since God
is, by hypothesis, always correct. Thus, Schleiermacher
would be correct to say that God's knowledge is no different

14. Friedrich Schleiermacher, *The Christian Faith,* ed. H. R.
Mackintosh and J. S. Stewart (Edinburgh, 1928), p. 228.

from that provided by an infallible prophet and, as a matter of fact, such knowledge would be quite sufficient to deny man's free will.

This leads us to another standard objection to the sort of proof I presented above. Maimonides put it this way:

> He obtains no new knowledge, He does not increase it, and it is not finite; nothing of all existing things escapes His knowledge, but their nature is not changed thereby; that which is possible remains possible. Every argument that seems to contradict any of these statements is founded on the nature of our knowledge, that has only the name in common with God's knowledge.[15]

This line of argument rests on the supposed significant differences between God's knowledge and our own, differences which are inexplicable since they are due to our lack of knowledge of God's attributes. In other words the word "know" has a different meaning when it is applied to God than when it is applied to man, and its meaning when applied to God is not entirely clear.

There is nothing necessarily incorrect about this reply,[16] but I believe that it is irrelevant to the issue at hand. The question which was originally posed was whether God's omniscience is logically incompatible with man's free will. God's omniscience was taken to be a knowledge of everything which is true. If it is objected that God's omniscience does not imply that He knows everything which is true, or that He knows it in some special way which provides an additional condition to the original definition of God's omniscience, this is not relevant to the point at issue. God may not be omniscient, or He may have a special sort of

15. Moses Maimonides, *The Guide For The Perplexed*, trans. M. Friedlander (London, 1928), p. 294.

16. I am purposely avoiding issues concerning the use of metaphor and analogy in religious language, since these issues are not relevant to the question of fatalism.

omniscience involving properties which we either cannot explain or which somewhat alter the usual definition of omniscience. What is at issue, however, is whether God's omniscience, as understood to mean simply that God knows everything which is true, is logically incompatible with free will. To deny that God is omniscient in this sense is simply to deny a premise whose truth is of no concern in this question.

Replies somewhat along the lines of that of Maimonides were made by Boethius, St. Anselm, and St. Thomas Aquinas. Boethius argued:

> since God lives in the eternal present, His knowledge transcends all movement of time and abides in the simplicity of its immediate present. It encompasses the infinite sweep of past and future, and regards all things in its simple comprehension as if they were now taking place. Thus, if you will think about the foreknowledge by which God distinguishes all things, you will rightly consider it to be not a foreknowledge of future events, but knowledge of a never changing present.[17]

St. Anselm argued similarly: "Thou wast not, then, yesterday, nor wilt thou be tomorrow; but yesterday and to-day and to-morrow thou art; or, rather, neither yesterday nor to-day nor to-morrow thou art; but simply, thou art, outside all time."[18] Aquinas also made this point, asserting, "Things reduced to act in time, are known by us successively in time but by God (are known) in eternity, which is above time."[19]

17. Boethius, *The Consolation of Philosophy,* trans. Richard Green (New York, 1962), Book 5, prose 6, p. 116.
18. St. Anselm, *Proslogium,* trans. S. W. Deane in *St. Anselm: Basic Writings* (La Salle, Illinois, 1962), Chap. 19, p. 25.
19. St. Thomas Aquinas, *Summa Theologica,* trans. Fathers of the English Dominican Province (London, 1920), q. 14, art. 13, p. 209.

In other words, God knows all things, whether past, present, or future, as present, and thus to speak of God's foreknowledge is misleading, since what appears to us to be foreknowledge is, in reality, knowledge of the present. Since man's knowledge of the present has no bearing on the problem of free will, so God's knowledge of the present similarly has no bearing on the problem of free will. As Boethius noted:

> Just as, when you happen to see simultaneously a man walking on the street and the sun shining in the sky, even though you see both at once, you can distinguish between them and realize that one action is voluntary, the other necessary; so the divine mind, looking down on all things, does not disturb the nature of the things which are present before it but are future with respect to time.[20]

But it is not at all clear what is meant by the thesis that God is "above time" or "outside of time." Whatever it means, it surely is not intended to deny that God knows every action which a man performs. But a man performs many actions which cannot be performed simultaneously. For instance, I raise my arm and I lower my arm but it is logically impossible that I perform both these actions at once. But if I do not perform both these actions at once, I must perform one before the other, and if God is omniscient he knows everything which is true and since it is true that I perform one action before I perform the other, God must know that I do this. How then are we to interpret the claim that God's knowledge "transcends all movement of time and abides in the . . . immediate present"?

If we wish to avoid redefining "knowledge" and thereby, as Maimonides did, evade but not answer the question of whether God's omniscience (using the word "omniscience" as commonly understood) is logically incompatible with

20. Boethius, p. 118.

man's free will, only one interpretation seems plausible. Whereas man views the future as unclear and, for the most part, unknown, God views the future as clearly as we view the present. This interpretation, however, though it is intelligible, does imply that God knows what I am going to do before I do it. It, therefore, constitutes no objection to my original proof and, indeed, it merely supports that proof, since it emphasizes the clarity and perfection of God's foreknowledge.

All of the objections discussed thus far have been intended to prove that the sort of argument I presented earlier is logically fallacious. There are those, however, who have not been convinced by these objections, even though they wish to affirm both God's omniscience and man's free will. William of Ockham, for instance, who was aware of the difficulty which God's omniscience presented to one who believed in future contingencies, argued that "it is impossible to describe clearly the way in which God knows future contingents. Nevertheless it must be held that He does so."[21] This "solution," though, is clearly unsatisfactory, since it amounts to the assertion that God is omniscient and that man has free will, but that how this can be logically possible is inexplicable.

At this point it seems obvious that for anyone who wishes to maintain logically that God is omniscient and that man has free will, only one alternative remains: viz. the denial of one of the premises of my proof. Petrus Aureoli, for instance, denied the law of excluded middle which is step (1) in the proof. He affirmed Aristotle's doctrine of future contingencies and maintained that a proposition affirming or

21. William Ockham, *Predestination, God's Foreknowledge, and Future Contingents,* trans. in an unpublished manuscript by N. Kretzmann and M. McCord of the University of Illinois, copyrighted in 1964, q. 1, P, p. 13. The Latin original can be found in Franciscan Institute Publications, no. 2, ed. Philotheus Boehner, New York, 1945.

denying that a contingent event will occur is neither true nor false. This would seem to imply that God does not foreknow whether a contingent event will occur, but Aureoli did not draw this conclusion. He noted that "foreknowledge does not make a proposition concerning a future contingent event a true proposition,"[22] and to that extent is consistent with the fact that such propositions are neither true nor false. He admitted, however, that God can only know true propositions, and thus it is not clear how God can know to be true a proposition which is neither true nor false. Aureoli realized this difficulty and admitted that "it is very difficult to find the right way of expressing the knowledge which God has of the future."[23]

Aureoli's position, however, is a good deal stronger than he seemed to have believed that it was, and, indeed, he is but one step from a solution to the supposed logical incompatibility between God's omniscience and man's free will. This step was, in fact, taken by a contemporary of Aureoli's, Levi ben Gersom (known as Gersonides). Gersonides directed his arguments against Maimonides' claim that we do not understand the nature of God's knowledge. Gersonides argues on the contrary that God's knowledge is like our own, except more perfect. Faced then with the seeming incompatibility between God's foreknowledge and man's free will, Gersonides, like Aureoli, adopted the Aristotelian view and argued that a proposition concerning a future contingency is neither true nor false.

In reply to the objection that this limited God's omniscience (the objection that had disturbed Aureoli), Gersonides replied that God is omniscient if He knows everything which is true. God does not know whether or not a contingent event will take place, but it is not true that a

22. Petrus Aureoli, *I Sententiarum* (Rome, 1596), 39, 3, p. 901, a C, quoted in Copleston, vol. 3, pt. 1, p. 50.

23. Ibid., p. 902, a F-b B, trans. in Copleston, p. 51.

contingent event will take place and it is not true that a
contingent event will not take place. What God *does* know
is which events are contingent and which, therefore, may
take place and may not take place. Indeed, it is logically
impossible for God to know whether a contingent event will
take place, for it is logically impossible to know what is not
true. This is no defect in God's knowledge for as Gersonides
puts it:

> When one has the potentiality[24] to do something then
> the accomplishment of the deed is considered a perfec-
> tion in him, since he has the potentiality over it, and
> when this potentiality is not realized, it would be re-
> garded a defect in him. But it could not be regarded a
> defect in him who has not the potentiality to accom-
> plish that deed, if that deed were not carried out by
> him.[25]

To take a specific example, assume that it is up to me
whether I will go swimming tomorrow. It is thus contingent
whether I will go swimming tomorrow. It is not true that I
will go swimming tomorrow, and it is not true that I will not
go swimming tomorrow. What *is* true is that I may go swimming tomorrow and I may not go swimming tomorrow. God
does not know whether I will go swimming tomorrow, but
this is no defect in God's knowledge, since it is not true that
I will go swimming tomorrow and it is not true that I will not
go swimming tomorrow. What God *does* know is that I
may go swimming tomorrow and I may not go swimming
tomorrow, and this is, in fact, the whole truth. If God knew
that I would go swimming tomorrow, He would know what
is not true, which is logically impossible. Similarly, if God

24. Potentiality is here to be taken as logical potentiality.
25. Levi ben Gersom, *The Commentary of Levi ben Gersom
(Gersonides) on the Book of Job*, trans. Abraham L. Lassen
(New York, 1946), p. 50.

knew that I would not go swimming tomorrow, He would
know what is not true, which is logically impossible. Thus,
to summarize Gersonides' position, God is omniscient since
He knows everything which is true. Nevertheless, man possesses free will since God does not know whether or not a
contingent event, such as a man's free action, will take place.

Gersonides' position has been championed recently by
Charles Hartshorne. He labels his view that "omniscience
sees the future as it is, that is, as partially indeterminate" as
the "Principle of Gersonides."[26] Hartshorne argues: "Igno-
rance is a lack of correspondence of knowledge to what is
known, a lack of adequacy to the subject. Indeterminism
justly denies any such lack in a mind's not knowing details
of a future which as future has not details to be known."[27]
In other words, since God knows everything that there is to
be known, He is omniscient although He does not know
whether or not a contingent event will take place.

Our discussion thus far has shown that if one wishes to
retain the law of excluded middle with regard to all propositions, he must either deny God's omniscience or deny man's
free will, for the two are logically incompatible. On the other
hand, one can assert both that God is omniscient and that
man has free will, *if* one is prepared to deny the law of excluded middle with regard to certain propositions, viz. those
that assert or deny, concerning a contingent event, that it is
going to occur.

But how is this related to the question of fatalism? Let
me now reformulate the proof which I originally presented
so as to eliminate all reference to theological matters, while
retaining the logical structure of the proof.

   (1) Every proposition must be either true, or if not
       true, then false.

26. Charles Hartshorne, *Man's Vision of God* (New York, 1941),
p. 139.
27. Ibid., p. 104.

(2) At t_1 (assume t_1 to be exactly one day earlier than t_2) it is true, or if not true, then false, that I will perform R at t_2.

(3) Assume that it is true at t_1 that I will perform R at t_2.

(4) But if it is true at t_1 that I will perform R at t_2, then if it is within my power to refrain from performing R at t_2, it would follow that it is within my power to confute the truth, i.e. it is within my power to make it true that what was *true* was also *false,* but this would imply that I could confute the law of contradiction, which is absurd.

(5) Therefore, it is not within my power to perform $\sim R$ at t_2.

(6) Assume next that it is false at t_1 that I will perform R at t_2.

(7) But if it is true at t_1 that I will not perform R at t_2, then if it is within my power to perform R at t_2, it would follow that it is within my power to confute the truth, i.e. it is within my power to make it true that what was *true* was also *false,* but this would imply that I could confute the law of contradiction, which is absurd.

(8) Therefore, it is not within my power to perform R at t_2.

(9) Thus, whether it is true at t_1 that I perform R at t_2 or whether it is false at t_1 that I perform R at t_2, R is not a free action.

A similar argument can be presented for any human action showing that it is not a free action, and thus fatalism is true.

One can, of course, avoid the conclusion of the second proof in the same manner as one can avoid the conclusion of the first proof, by denying step (1), the law of excluded middle, as it applies to those propositions that assert or deny, concerning a contingent event, that it is going to occur.

If it was not true yesterday that I would perform R today, and if it was also not false yesterday that I would perform R today, it does not follow that R is not a free action. However, this second proof does seem to show that one can avoid fatalism only by affirming that there are certain propositions to which the law of excluded middle does not apply.

We shall next turn to a modern argument for fatalism, one that differs considerably from those discussed thus far. This modern argument has caused great stir, and it is to my mind one of the most subtle arguments that has ever been offered in support of fatalism.

6 A Modern View of Fatalism

Most contemporary philosophers who have discussed the problem of fatalism have done so in order either to clarify just what it was that Aristotle, Diodorus Cronus, Ockham, or some other previous philosopher actually thought about fatalism or to demonstrate just what is wrong with the traditional proofs of fatalism. There is at least one major exception to this generalization, however, and that is the work of Richard Taylor, who not only has supported certain traditional arguments for fatalism but also has constructed a new proof of this most controversial thesis.[1] The following chapter deals with this new proof and the criticisms directed against it.[2]

Taylor's proof rests on six premises, each of which he believes to be accepted by almost all philosophers.[3] Let us examine each of these six premises in turn.

(1) Every proposition is either true, or, if not true, then false. This is the traditional law of excluded middle.

1. Richard Taylor, "Fatalism," *The Philosophical Review, 71* (1962), 56–66; "Fatalism and Ability," *Analysis, 24* (1962), 25–27; "A Note on Fatalism," *The Philosophical Review, 72* (1963), 497–99; "Comment," *The Journal of Philosophy, 61* (1964), 305–07. Taylor's views are summarized in *Metaphysics* (Englewood Cliffs, N.J , 1963), pp. 54–69.

2. This chapter is a revised version of my paper "Fatalistic Arguments," *The Journal of Philosophy, 61* (1964), 295–305.

3. It should be emphasized at the outset that in all his writings Taylor has never claimed to prove fatalism as such. He claims only that certain commonly held assumptions, to which he is not necessarily committed, yield a proof of fatalism.

(2) If one state of affairs (A) is sufficient for the occurrence of another state of affairs (B), then A cannot occur without B occurring, even though the two are logically unconnected. This, Taylor claims, is the "standard way" in which the concept of sufficiency is explained in philosophy. The absence of oxygen is thus sufficient for the absence of human life, which means simply that if there is no oxygen present, there can be no human life.

(3) If one state of affairs (B) is necessary for the occurrence of another state of affairs (A), then A cannot occur unless B occurs, even though the two are logically unconnected. This, Taylor claims, is the "standard way" in which the concept of a necessary condition is explained in philosophy. The presence of oxygen is thus a necessary condition for the presence of human life, which means simply that human life cannot exist without oxygen.

(4) If one state of affairs (A) is sufficient for the occurrence of another state of affairs (B), then B is necessary for A. Conversely, if A is necessary for B, then B is sufficient for A. This is a logical consequence of premises (2) and (3).

(5) No agent can perform a particular action (A) if there is lacking at any time a necessary condition for A. This follows from the definition of a necessary condition presented in premise (3). For instance, I cannot live without the presence of oxygen.[4]

---

4 Taylor's fifth premise is slightly mistaken. It should read "No agent can perform a particular action (A) if there is lacking at any time a necessary condition for an agent's being able to perform A." Since this alteration in no way affects the ultimate validity of Taylor's argument (though it would necessitate certain alterations in his proofs), I will assume his formulation to be correct and answer objections to his proof in terms of his own formulation. His mistake only becomes significant when one tries to avoid his fatalistic conclusion by suspending the law of excluded middle. Given his formulation of the fifth premise, the suspension of the law of excluded middle leads to the conclusion that no action whatever is possible. See my proof in "Fatalistic Arguments," pp. 293–95 and Taylor's

(6) The mere passage of time does not increase or decrease the capacities of anything or anyone. Thus, as a man ages and loses his power to run rapidly, it is not the passage of time which causes him to lose his power, but rather some changes in his physical structure.[5]

It is Taylor's claim that if one grants these six premises then he is thereby logically committed to fatalism. Taylor's method of proof consists of two stages. In the first stage he claims to prove that fatalism is true with regard to all past events: we can do nothing to alter the past. In the second stage he claims to prove in an identical manner that fatalism is true with regard to all future events: we can do nothing to alter the future. Let us examine each of these proofs in turn.

PROOF I   Assume that the occurrence of a naval battle yesterday is a necessary condition for my reading a headline today confirming the occurrence of that naval battle. Call the two propositions "A naval battle occurred yesterday" and "No naval battle occurred yesterday" P and P′ respectively. Call my reading a headline today confirming the occurrence of the naval battle S. Call my not reading such a headline today S′. Taylor asks us to consider whether the statement (A) "It is now within my power to do S, and it is also now

---

"Comment," p. 307. Charles Hartshorne, in his article "Deliberation and Excluded Middle," *The Journal of Philosophy, 61* (1964), 476–77, claims that my proof is "sophistical." But he then goes on to imply that if Taylor's premises were accepted, my proof would be sound. This is, of course, exactly what I wished to show. Hartshorne also suggests how Taylor can alter his fifth premise so as to avoid the force of my proof, and I have formalized Hartshorne's suggestion above.

5. It may be recalled that Copleston's reconstruction of Diodorus' Master Argument was rejected because it utilized a premise, very similar to Taylor's sixth premise, which could be reasonably denied. The subtlety of Taylor's argument is that to avoid its fatalistic conclusion, it is not enough to deny the sixth premise. One must also deny the first premise, the law of excluded middle, and this is a step which many are reluctant to take.

within my power to do S'" is true. He believes that it is not true and utilizes the following proof:

> 1. If P is true, then it is not within my power to do S' (for in case P is true, then there is, or was, lacking a condition essential for my doing S', the condition, namely, of there being no naval battle yesterday).
>
> 2. But if P' is true, then it is not within my power to do S (for a similar reason).
>
> 3. But either P is true or P' is true.
>
> 4. Either it is not within my power to do S, or it is not within my power to do S'; and A is accordingly false.[6]

In other words, which headline I see depends, among other things, on whether a naval battle took place yesterday, and since that is not now up to me, it is not now up to me which headline I read.

PROOF II   Assume that I am a naval commander who is about to issue the order of the day, and assume that my issuing one sort of order is a sufficient condition for the occurrence of a naval battle tomorrow, whereas my issuing another sort of order is a sufficient condition for there being no naval battle tomorrow. Call the two propositions "A naval battle will occur tomorrow" and "No naval battle will occur tomorrow" Q and Q' respectively. Call my issuing an order ensuring a naval battle tomorrow O and call my issuing an order ensuring no naval battle tomorrow O'. Assume that O or O' is a forced option. Taylor asks us to consider whether the statement (B) "It is now within my power to do O, and it is also now within my power to do O'" is true. He believes that it is not true and utilizes the following proof:

> 1. If Q is true, then it is not within my power to do O' (for in case Q is true, then there is, or will be, lacking a

6. Taylor, *Metaphysics,* p. 60.

condition essential for my doing O', the condition, namely, of there being no naval battle tomorrow).

2. But if Q' is true, then it is not within my power to do O (for a similar reason).

3. But either Q is true or Q' is true.

4. Either it is not within my power to do O, or it is not within my power to do O'; and B is accordingly false.[7]

In other words, which order I issue depends, among other things, on whether a naval battle will take place tomorrow, and since that is not now up to me (since before I issue my order, it is already true, or if not true, then false, that a naval battle will take place tomorrow), it is not now up to me which order I issue.

Considering the fact that any action anyone does is sufficient for certain occurrences in the future, it follows that these occurrences are necessary conditions of the present action and thus the second proof can be generalized to yield the conclusion that for any act A whatsoever, either it is not within one's power to do A, or it is not within one's power not to do A, depending on which consequences are, in fact, going to ensue.

Taylor's argument has drawn critical comment from many quarters.[8] In what follows, I propose to show that these replies are inconclusive, that the most crucial point in the argument has been entirely overlooked, and that it is on this point that Taylor's argument must stand or fall.

7. Ibid., p. 60.

8. John Turk Saunders, "Professor Taylor on Fatalism," *Analysis, 23* (1962), 1–2; Bruce Aune, "Fatalism and Professor Taylor," *The Philosophical Review, 71* (1962), 512–19; Peter Makepeace, "Fatalism and Ability, II," *Analysis, 23* (1962), 27–29; John Turk Saunders, "Fatalism and Linguistic Reform," ibid., 30–31; Raziel Abelson, "Taylor's Fatal Fallacy," *The Philosophical Review, 72* (1963), 93–96; Richard Sharvy, "A Logical Error in Taylor's 'Fatalism,'" *Analysis, 23* (1963), 96; John Turk Saunders, "Fatalism and

John Turk Saunders denies that Taylor's arguments, even
if accepted, are sufficient to prove fatalism, since for that
purpose Taylor would have to show that (S), "Every act of
every agent is such that all alternative acts have lacking at
least one future necessary condition," and Taylor has not
shown this.[9] Indeed, Saunders claims that Taylor cannot do
this, since S is not a meaningful statement and fatalism is,
therefore, not a *"meaningful* doctrine." Saunders is correct
in asserting that Taylor assumes S without attempting to
prove it; however, Saunders is in error, I believe, in asserting
that S is not a meaningful statement.

Let P represent the performance of some particular action. Let $\sim$P represent the nonperformance of that same
particular action. P is sufficient for the situation being such
that the day after P occurs, no one has it within his power to
prevent the occurrence of P.[10] Thus, no one having it within
his power the day after P occurs to prevent the occurrence of
P is a necessary condition for P. Similarly, $\sim$P is sufficient
for the situation being such that the day after $\sim$P occurs, no
one has it within his power to prevent the occurrence of $\sim$P.
Thus, no one having it within his power the day after P
occurs to prevent the occurrence of $\sim$P is a necessary condition for $\sim$P. According to the law of excluded middle,
either P occurs or $\sim$P occurs. If P occurs then a future
necessary condition is lacking for $\sim$P; if $\sim$P occurs then a
future necessary condition is lacking for P. In either case
a future necessary condition is lacking for all alternative

---

the Logic of 'Ability,' " ibid (1963), 24; Richard Sharvy, "Tautology
and Fatalism," *The Journal of Philosophy, 61* (1964), 293–95; John
Turk Saunders, "Fatalism and Ordinary Language," *The Journal of
Philosophy, 62* (1965), 211–22; Charles D. Brown, "Fallacies in
Taylor's 'Fatalism,' " *The Journal of Philosophy, 62* (1965), 349–53.

9. Saunders, "Fatalism and Ordinary Language," p. 212.

10. The terms "necessary," "sufficient," and "prevent" are used
here in the sense explicated in Chapter 3.

acts. The same proof would, of course, hold for any particular action. Thus, (S) is not, as Saunders would have us believe, meaningless. Quite to the contrary, S is both meaningful and undeniably true.

Taylor has also been criticized for equivocating in the use of the term "can." Saunders, for example, suggests that Taylor confuses logical impossibility with "not having the power to." The presupposition that no agent can perform any action in the absence of some condition necessary for its accomplishment expresses, according to Saunders, only a certain innocuous logical impossibility, and thus has nothing to do with what any agent is able to do. He argues that:

> My knocking upon a thin wooden door with my fist is a sufficient condition for the door's shaking. Hence the door's shaking is a necessary condition for my knocking upon the door. But the door's shaking is not a necessary condition for my ability to knock upon the door.[11]

Taylor, however, did not argue that no agent can know how to perform some act in the absence of some condition necessary for its accomplishment, and thus, in that sense, does not have the ability to perform it. His point was, rather, that no matter what an agent might know how to do, he still cannot even do what he knows how to do (and is in that sense able to do) if there is lacking some condition necessary for doing it.

For example, imagine an expert pole-vaulter locked up in a room with an eight-foot ceiling. Both Taylor and Saunders might agree that an expert pole-vaulter has technical expertise to pole-vault twelve feet. In this sense of the word "can" the pole-vaulter can pole-vault twelve feet. What Taylor is asserting is that, given the conditions of the locked room, the pole-vaulter does not have it within his

11. Saunders, "Professor Taylor on Fatalism," p. 2.

power to pole-vault twelve feet. His know-how is constrained by circumstances that prevent him from exercising it.

Bruce Aune makes a point similar to Saunders'. Aune claims that Taylor's presupposition that no agent can perform any given action if there is lacking some condition necessary for the accomplishment of that action, has "absurd consequences." As an example he suggests the following:

> If a man should say that he can swim, or that he has the ability to swim, he would surely take it as a poor joke if someone replied, 'No, you cannot swim: you lack the ability to do this because you are not now in a pool or lake.'[12]

To this we should reply that if a man should say that he can swim, or that he has the ability to swim, he would surely take it as a poor joke if someone said, "Well, then, you can swim under any conditions. Let's see you swim out of water." The first of these "jokes" is not a joke at all, since, in one sense, it simply states an obvious truth, namely, that one needs water in order to swim, and it is precisely in that sense that Taylor utilizes it. The second "joke" is indeed a joke, since it assumes that when a man says that he can swim, he means that he can swim at a specific time even if conditions necessary for his swimming then are lacking. Of course, no man takes this to be the meaning of the sentence "I can swim." What one means is that he is able to swim at any specific time if all other conditions necessary for his swimming are then present, and such conditions obviously include the presence of water. Again, Taylor's use of "can" seems perfectly legitimate and is not a distortion of common usage.

Saunders, in a reply to Taylor, alters his position somewhat and denies that "no agent has the power to perform

12. Aune, p. 514.

an act a past necessary condition of which is lacking." He asserts that this is not always true since, for example, "my not deciding at t_2 not to swim at t_3 is a necessary condition of my swimming at t_3 whose absence does not render me powerless to swim at t_3."[13] Saunders' claim that my decision at t_2 to swim at t_3 is a necessary condition of my swimming at t_3 seems untenable, since I could get pushed into the pool at t_3 despite my previous decision not to swim. But even if my decision at t_2 *were,* in fact, a necessary condition of my swimming at t_3—a condition in the absence of which my swimming at t_3 is impossible—and I do *not* make that decision at t_2, then at t_3 it is not within my power to go swimming. If it were within my power to go swimming at t_3, then I would have it within my power to do what Saunders agrees is impossible, to alter the past, for I would have it within my power to alter my decision or lack of it at t_2.

Saunders also asserts that if I decided at t_2 to do S at t_3 and this decision is sufficient for S at t_3, then at t_3 I am still free with regard to S. But even if my decision at t_2 *were,* in fact, a sufficient condition of my swimming at t_3—a condition given which my not swimming at t_3 is impossible—and I *do* make that decision at t_2, then at t_3 it is not within my power not to go swimming. If it were within my power not to go swimming at t_3, then I would have it within my power once again to do what Saunders agrees is impossible, to alter the past, for I would have it within my power to alter my decision at t_2.

Some critics have, in effect, pointed out that Taylor's arguments lead to fatalism. Saunders, for example, dismisses it as strange that "my mere ability to knock upon the door will suffice to make it shake." This, however, is simply part of the fatalist position. I cannot perform a given act if there is lacking a condition necessary for doing it, no matter what I might know how to do, and this does indeed imply, as

13. Saunders, "Fatalism and Ordinary Language," p. 216.

Saunders points out, that if I can knock on the door then I shall. However strange this may seem, it is only because fatalism is strange, and it is hardly a criticism that Taylor's argument, which purports to yield a fatalist conclusion, does yield such a conclusion.

Peter Makepeace's comments are in some respects similar. Like Saunders, he appears to allow Taylor's argument while disputing claims not made by Taylor. He agrees that "I cannot make something happen in the future if it is not going to happen." But this is just Taylor's conclusion; it is logically equivalent to saying that if it is true that a certain event *e* is not going to happen, then I cannot make it happen—to which we can add that, if it is false that the event in question is not going to happen, then I cannot prevent it from happening. And this is fatalism.

What, then, does Makepeace dispute? He introduces the following example:

> If conditions are such that a snowfall yesterday is a necessary condition for the lawn's being snow-covered this morning, then, given that no snowfall occurred, we can conclude not only that the lawn *is not* snow-covered, but that it *cannot* be.[14]

He then claims that we ought not to speak of the lawn's state of being snow-covered as not being "within its power," and that it is "absurd" to add that this "is consistent with its being able to carry snow, having the ability not to melt it, and so on, and thus being able, in *that* sense."

This, however, is not absurd; it is only an odd choice of words. Makepeace is rightly reluctant to use 'within its power' in connection with inanimate objects. But this is a minor point. If he wishes to change the examples from animate to inanimate objects, Taylor can change the expression 'within his power' to 'within its capability.' Now, we

14. Makepeace, p. 28.

find Makepeace repeating Saunders' error by disputing what Taylor has not claimed. Taylor has not claimed that the lawn does not possess the capability to hold snow (to carry snow, to melt it, and so on), any more than he claims that the pole-vaulter does not have the know-how to pole-vault twelve feet in a room with an eight-foot-high ceiling.

What Taylor can rightly claim is that, given the absence of a necessary condition, the lawn does not have it within its capability to be snow-covered, just as the pole-vaulter does not have it within his power to pole-vault twelve feet. And this, it would appear, is just what Makepeace admits when he concludes "I cannot make something happen in the future if it is not going to happen." Certainly, if I can't do it, neither can a lawn.

In a further criticism, Saunders accuses Taylor of re-defining 'within one's power' while still employing it in its usual contexts. It is this "linguistic reform," he claims, that accounts for the seeming fatalistic conclusion of Taylor's argument. Taylor, according to Saunders, treats it as analytic that "the only events which it is within one's power to produce are those which occur."

Taylor does not treat this statement as analytic. It does, however, follow from his argument, and it leads to the conclusion that the only actions one is able to perform are those which he does perform—which is, again, the conclusion of fatalism.

Does this, however, amount to a linguistic reform? It seems not. Consider a violinist, for instance, who has forgotten to bring his violin to his recital and is unable to obtain another before the time of the recital. What Taylor is *not* asserting is that this violinist could not play the violin at his recital even if he had a violin in his hands. Such an assertion would be patently false. What he *is* asserting is that if at the time of the recital the violinist does not have a violin to play, then he cannot at that time present a recital, for he cannot play an imaginary violin. This statement, in contrast to the previous one, is obviously true, and in a perfectly ordinary sense of "cannot."

Taylor admits that there is another sense to the word "can" which he does not utilize. This is the notion of know-how. There is a sense of the word 'can' such that it is true that the violinist without his violin can still play the violin, since he knows how to. Taylor does not use this sense of 'can,' however, since if this sense were to be utilized, fatalism with respect to the past would also be shown to be false.

Assume, for instance, that a sufficient condition of my having gone to a lecture yesterday is my having my own notes from it. Suppose that yesterday I did not go to the lecture. According to Taylor's use of the word 'can,' this implies that I cannot perform any act today sufficient for my having gone to the lecture yesterday—that it is not within my power today to read my notes from that lecture, since no such notes exist. No one doubts this, for we are all fatalists with respect to the past. We would not be led to alter our beliefs with respect to the past if someone argued similarly to Saunders, that I really *can* perform an act sufficient for my having gone to the lecture yesterday, that I really *can* read my notes from it, since I now *know how* to read, to open my notebook, and so on. No one accepts that meaning of "can" with respect to the past.

What Taylor has done is to disregard that meaning of 'can' with respect to the future also. He would claim that, if it is true that I will not go to the lecture today, then I cannot perform any act sufficient for my attending it, and this is consistent with my knowing how to walk to the lecture hall, find a seat there, and so on. Saunders' seemingly plausible claim that one can sometimes do something sufficient for the future occurrence of what is not going to happen is in fact no more reasonable than the absurd claim that one can sometimes do something sufficient for the past occurrence of what did not happen.

Taylor has not engaged in linguistic reform. Rather, he

has utilized one sense of 'can' which, in regard to the past, is consistent with everyone's use of that word. What he has tried to show is that this sense ought to be just as consistent with everyone's use of the word in regard to the future, though this is not the case, since people are not aware of their limitations with respect to the future but only with respect to the past.

In a reply Taylor suggests that if Saunders' argument does indeed refute fatalism in respect to the future, then it also refutes fatalism in respect to the past.[15] Saunders denies this and asserts:

> if the non-occurrence of an event in the future does not entail my lack of power to bring about that event, then neither does the non-occurrence of an event in the past entail my lack of power to bring about that event . . . but it is not due to the non-occurrence of an event in the past that I lack the power to bring about that event. I have no such power because we so use our language that it is false or nonsense to say that one has the power to bring about any event whatever in the past.[16]

But this does not at all seem to answer Taylor's charge. An expression possesses what meaning is conferred by its use. The question why it is used as it is still remains. Has it an arbitrary use? Or is there some actual difference between the past and the future which would account for making this distinction? If Saunders wishes to answer Taylor's charge he must point out such a difference, for it is the denial of such a difference upon which Taylor's argument essentially rests.

It has also been suggested that Taylor confuses causally necessary conditions with logical necessity. Raziel Abelson, for example, suggests that, if the states of affairs described

15. Taylor, "Fatalism and Ability," pp. 26–27.
16. Saunders, "Fatalism and Linguistic Reform," p. 31.

in Taylor's argument are not logically related, they must be causally related. This is not quite correct, however, since Taylor expresses his argument entirely in terms of necessary and sufficient conditions which, unlike causal conditions, involve no temporal relations at all. If, for instance, the presence of oxygen is a necessary condition of a certain man's being alive over a given period of time, then that man's continuing to live over that period is a sufficient condition for there being oxygen present. But neither of these is logically necessary or sufficient for the other, nor is either the cause of the other. The presence of oxygen may be a causal condition of that man's continuing to live, but certainly his living is no causal condition for the presence of oxygen—even though it is a sufficient condition for the presence of oxygen.

Aune, on the other hand, criticizes Taylor for excluding logically necessary and sufficient conditions from his examples and for formulating his argument entirely in terms of what Aune labels "physically" necessary and sufficient conditions. He points out that logical necessity implies physical necessity and that the introduction of logical necessity into the argument has a damaging effect upon it.

He is quite right in noting that Taylor has chosen to deal only with "physically" necessary or sufficient conditions which are not also logically necessary or sufficient conditions, but not right in suggesting that Taylor denies that logical necessity implies "physical" necessity. Taylor takes no stand on this, which is, in fact, not relevant to his argument. Likewise irrelevant is the claim that his argument, if expressed in terms of logically necessary or sufficient conditions, leads to the abolishment of all modal distinctions. It is no more to the point to criticize Taylor's arguments for ignoring logically necessary or sufficient conditions than to criticize it for ignoring causal conditions, for the question is not whether other, more or less similar, arguments yield a fatalistic conclusion, but whether Taylor's argument does.

Abelson claims that Taylor's assumption that time is not efficacious is ambiguous, since, he says, time is logically efficacious. Here Abelson seems simply to misunderstand Taylor's notion of the efficacy of time. Taylor explains this by noting that the mere passage of time does not augment or diminish the powers or capacities of anything. Abelson, however, seems to equate the sentence "Time is logically efficacious" with the sentence "Time often has a lot to do with the truth of what we say." But these two sentences are entirely different. For instance, the sentence "It is now raining" may be true today and false tomorrow. Quite obviously, time has a lot to do with the truth of the sentence. But it is not time which augmented the power of the clouds to produce rain. Certain meteorological conditions did that. Time in this sense is not efficacious.

Aune also criticizes this assumption, but somewhat differently. He notes that time cannot pass without something changing. This is doubtless true, but it has nothing to do with Taylor's assumption, which says only that the passage of time "has no causal effect upon anything." Perhaps something must change during any period of time, but it is not time which causes such change. A lake, for example, is dried up, not by time, but by certain meteorological conditions or by emptying the lake. This happens in time, to be sure, but time by itself is no cause of it.

Some critics have suggested that Taylor has simply misplaced certain modal concepts, which is a fairly common fallacy. Taylor's crucial assumption, for example, is that no agent can perform any action in the absence of some condition necessary for its accomplishment. But, according to these critics, all this really means is that it (logically) cannot be the case that an agent *does* perform an action in the absence of some condition necessary for its accomplishment —which is perfectly compatible with saying that he can perform such an action.

Thus Abelson accuses Taylor of committing a fallacy

which "lies at the root of the famous paradox of Chrysippus: a man necessarily does X or does not do X (excluded middle). Therefore either he necessarily does X or he necessarily does not do X."[17] In this argument the necessity of the logical truth of the first statement is illicitly transferred from the entire disjunction to the individual disjuncts.

However, it appears that Abelson has committed a similar error in reverse. Taylor's argument can be interpreted, with certain qualifications, as saying that if A, then necessarily B, and if ~B, then necessarily ~A. Abelson transfers these individual necessities to the necessity of the entire proposition "If A implies B, and ~B, then ~A." This proposition is logically true, as is the first statement of the Chrysippus paradox. But whereas that paradox asserts a second statement which does not logically follow from the first, Abelson denies a second statement which, in fact, is the premise from which his first statement is deduced. What Abelson does is to transfer the necessity of two individual implications to the necessity of a logical truth which follows from these two individual implications. He is not logically in error in doing so, but then he refuses to acknowledge the necessity of the two individual implications, since they do not follow from the necessity of the logical truth. This is somewhat like the Chrysippus paradox in reverse.

Aune also criticizes Taylor's use of modal concepts, but somewhat differently. He says that if Taylor's crucial assumption, to the effect that no agent can perform any action in the absence of some condition necessary for its accomplishment, is "taken as a necessary truth" or "a result of logical analysis," then the statements (i) "he performs A," (ii) "he can perform A," and (iii) "he has to perform A" are all logically equivalent. All that follows from Taylor's assumption, however, is that these statements are *extensionally* equivalent, not that they are *logically* equivalent.

17. Abelson, p. 95.

To assert their extensional equivalence, however, is only to assert fatalism, which does indeed follow from Taylor's argument. If I can perform A, then I do, in fact, perform A, and moreover, I must. This is a strange conclusion only if one happens to reject fatalism. To point out that it is strange is only to reject the conclusion; it is not to refute it.

It seems to me that if Taylor's argument is faulty, the fault lies much deeper than these critics have believed. It is not a comparatively simple matter of linguistic reform or modal fallacies. Rather, the whole nature of the laws of logic is brought into question.

7 Fatalism and the Laws of Logic

I have thus far concluded that certain proofs of fatalism (two proofs suggested by Aristotle, Arthur Prior's reconstruction of Diodorus' Master Argument, my proof derived from certain theological considerations, and Richard Taylor's proof) are sound *if* one accepts the law of excluded middle—the premise that every proposition must be either true, or if not true, then false (of course, one must also accept the other laws of logic enumerated in Chapter 1). However, each of these proofs fails if one holds that the law of excluded middle does not apply to certain propositions concerning future contingent events. In what follows I intend to examine the law of excluded middle and discuss what reasons there are for accepting a law which logically implies fatalism.

The law of excluded middle is one of the three so-called "laws of thought," the other two being the law of identity (if any proposition is true, it is true) and the law of contradiction (if any proposition is true, its contradictory must be false). Aristotle, who first formalized these laws, believed them to "hold good for everything that is,"[1] and he maintained that they were necessary truths and not merely hypotheses, for "a principle which every one must have who understands anything that is, is not a hypothesis."[2] Although few, if any, thinkers have doubted the fundamental importance of these laws, there has been much dispute, espe-

1. Aristotle, *Metaphysics*, 1005^a 24.
2. Ibid., 1005^b 15–17.

cially during the twentieth century, concerning their precise status.

There are those who argue that the laws of thought describe the fundamental structure of all actual and possible objects in the world. Morris Raphael Cohen, for instance, argues that these laws "apply to nature because they describe the invariant relations which are found in it."[3] Bertrand Russell argues similarly that these laws are "fact[s] concerning the things in the world" and are "applicable to whatever the world may contain, both what is mental and what is non-mental."[4] This position is also defended by Brand Blanshard, who notes: "Why should we shrink from saying that p and its contradictory, that this crow is black and that it is not black, are both true? To which the simple and sufficient answer is: Because the crow itself cannot have incompatible attributes, and we see that it cannot."[5]

There are those thinkers, however, who argue that the laws of thought tell us nothing whatever about the structure of actual and possible objects in the world. C. I. Lewis, for instance, argues that the laws of logic are accepted "on pragmatic grounds of conformity to human bent and intellectual convenience."[6] Ernest Nagel argues similarly that the laws of thought

> specify minimal conditions for discourse without confusion, for they state at least some of the requirements for a precise language . . . It must nevertheless be acknowledged that the ideal of precision in using language is not an arbitrary one. It is not arbitrary because

3. Morris R. Cohen, *Reason and Nature* (Glencoe, 1953), p. 204.

4. Bertrand Russell, *The Problems of Philosophy* (New York, 1959), p. 89.

5. Brand Blanshard, *Reason and Analysis* (London, 1962), p. 425.

6. Clarence Irving Lewis, "A Pragmatic Conception of the *a Priori*," in Feigl and Sellars, eds , *Readings in Philosophical Analysis* (New York, 1949), p. 288.

communication, and inquiry in particular, is directed
to the achievement of certain objectives, and these
objectives are best obtained when language is employed in a manner approximating as closely as possible to the norms expressed by the laws of thought.[7]

This general position is also defended by A. J. Ayer, who
notes:

if I say, "Nothing can be coloured in different ways at
the same time with respect to the same part of itself,"
I am not saying anything about the properties of any
actual thing . . . I am expressing an analytical proposition which records our determination to call a colour
expanse which differs in quality from a neighboring
colour expanse a different part of a given thing.[8]

The position defended by Cohen, Russell, and Blanshard
(which I shall henceforth refer to as the "ontological view")
and the position defended by Lewis, Nagel, and Ayer (which
I shall henceforth refer to as the "pragmatic view") have at
least one thing in common: they both assume the truth of
the law of excluded middle. But what precisely is the law
of excluded middle? Aristotle formulated it this way: "there
cannot be an intermediate between contradictories, but of
one subject we must either affirm or deny any one predi-
cate."[9]

But this is not an entirely clear formulation of the law
of excluded middle. Consider, for instance, the following
two formulations of that law: (1) every proposition must be
either true or false, i.e. for any interpretation of P, "$P \lor \sim P$"
is true; (2) every proposition must be either true, or if not

7. Ernest Nagel, *Logic Without Metaphysics* (Glencoe, 1956),
pp. 74–75.

8. A J Ayer, *Language, Truth and Logic* (second ed. New York,
1946), p 79.

9. Aristotle, *Metaphysics,* 1011[b] 24.

true, then false, i.e. for any interpretation of P, "P" is true or "$\sim P$" is true.[10] Both these formulations may appear to express what Aristotle had in mind by the law of excluded middle, and yet it does not seem to me that (1) and (2) have the same meaning or that Aristotle would have accepted both (1) and (2). However, before I go on to explain why I do not believe (1) and (2) are equivalent, let us assume that (1) and (2) are equivalent and see what the consequences are for the ontological view of the laws of thought and for the pragmatic view of the laws of thought.

If (1) and (2) are equivalent formulations of the law of excluded middle, then, as has been shown in the previous chapters, they both logically imply fatalism. Those who hold the ontological view are thus logically committed to fatalism. This, however, is not an entirely implausible result of the ontological view, since this view maintains that the law of excluded middle does express a basic truth about the world which we cannot alter and must therefore accept.

On the other hand, those who hold the pragmatic view can assert that since the law of excluded middle logically commits one to fatalism, they choose in some cases not to employ this law. This is consistent with the pragmatic view, since this view holds that the law of excluded middle is simply the most convenient method of organizing language, and there is no reason always to adopt the most convenient method of organizing language. But is it possible that simply by adopting a linguistic convention, one can thereby be committed to the thesis that no man has free will? This is surely absurd. Of course, if one arbitrarily decides to use the terms "is immortal" and "has free will" as synonymous, one could by linguistic convention alone find oneself committed to the thesis that no man "has free will," but this sort of linguistic convention would not alter the truth-value

10. The verbal formulations of (1) and (2) are no doubt less clear than the symbolic formulations. Nevertheless the verbal formulations seem the best available.

of what is usually expressed by the statement "no man has free will." Indeed, it appears that on the pragmatic view an analytic proposition, viz. the law of excluded middle, logically implies a synthetic proposition, viz. no man has free will.[11] But this is impossible and thus if (1) and (2) are equivalent, the pragmatic view is untenable. But are (1) and (2) equivalent propositions?

Let us consider the propositions symbolized by "P" and "$\sim P$," the first of which affirms, concerning a contingent event, that it will occur, and the second of which denies that the event in question will occur. Aristotle argued that concerning P and $\sim P$, "one of the two propositions . . . must be true and the other false, but we cannot say determinately that this or that is false, but must leave the alternative undecided."[12] In other words Aristotle argued that $(P \vee \sim P)$ is necessarily true, but P is not true and $\sim P$ is not true.[13]

Aristotle's view, however, has been severely criticized. Quine refers to "the desperate extremity of entertaining Aristotle's fantasy that 'It is true that p or q' is an insufficient condition for 'It is true that p or it is true that q.' "[14] Donald Williams calls Aristotle's reasoning "so swaggeringly invalid that the student can hardly believe he meant it," and his

11 For my purposes an analytic statement is "a statement which is true and remains true under all reinterpretations of its components other than the logical particles." This definition is provided in Willard V O. Quine, *From a Logical Point of View* (New York, 1953), pp 22–23

12. Aristotle, *De Int.,* 19ª, 36–37. The quotation could be rendered in the following way to clarify its meaning· "one of the two propositions   must be true . . . but we cannot say determinately that this or that is [true], but must leave the alternative undecided."

13 The reader is reminded that it would be historically safer to attribute these views to a "commonly accepted interpretation of Aristotle."

14. Willard V. O Quine, "On a So-Called Paradox," *Mind, 62* (1953), 65.

conclusion "as nearly incredible as any proposition could be."[15] Similarly, Leonard Linsky claims that the view that "T(S v ~S) & ~T(S) & ~T(~S)" is "absurd."[16]

I intend to show, however, that far from being absurd, Aristotle's view is profound and that if his position is taken seriously and its implications are clearly understood, it will be seen to yield a solution to the problem of fatalism.

If it is necessarily true that every proposition must be either true or false, does it follow that every proposition must be either true, or if not true, then false? To take a specific example, assume that I will arrive at a fork in the road and must either take one road (call my taking that road "R") or take the other road (call my taking that road "$\sim R$"). It is logically necessary that I will do R or $\sim R$. But does this imply that it is true that I will do R, or if it is not true that I will do R, then it is true that I will do $\sim R$? Before trying to answer this question, let us examine two somewhat analogous questions.

Assume that it is logically necessary that I will do R or $\sim R$. Does it follow that it is logically necessary that I will do R, or that if it is not logically necessary that I will do R, then it is logically necessary that I will do $\sim R$? In order to view this question symbolically, let "LN" stand for logical necessity and "v" for exclusive alternation. The question then is this: does $LN(R$ v $\sim R)$ imply $LN(R)$ v $[\sim LN(R) \supset LN(\sim R)]$? This can be simplified to the following question: does $LN(R$ v $\sim R)$ imply $LN(R)$ v $LN(\sim R)$? The answer seems quite clearly to be no. It is a well-known fact of modal logic that the logical necessity of a disjunction does not imply the logical necessity of its individual disjuncts. For example, though it is logically

15. Williams, pp. 284, 291.

16. Leonard Linsky, "Professor Donald Williams on Aristotle," *The Philosophical Review, 63* (1954), 250–51. The "T" in Linsky's notation stands for "true."

necessary that either I always exist or I do not always exist, this does not imply that either I am a necessarily existent being or that I am a necessarily nonexistent being. Thus, $LN(R \vee \sim R)$ does not imply $LN(R) \vee LN(\sim R)$.

Assume again that it is logically necessary that I will do R or $\sim R$. Does it follow that it is physically necessary[17] that I will do R, or that if it is not physically necessary that I will do R, then it is physically necessary that I will do $\sim R$? In order to view this question symbolically, let "PN" stand for physical necessity. The question then is this: does $LN(R \vee \sim R)$ imply $PN(R) \vee PN(\sim R)$? The answer again seems to be no. To bring out this point clearly assume that I cannot do R (perhaps because the road is too steep) and that it is therefore physically necessary that I will do $\sim R$. In this case it is logically necessary that I will do R or $\sim R$, and it is also physically necessary that I will do $\sim R$. But no such special circumstance, viz. that I cannot do R, was present in the original question. It was simply logically necessary that I would do R or $\sim R$. This implies nothing concerning whether it is physically necessary that I will do R or whether it is physically necessar' that I will do $\sim R$. It may be within my power to do R and it may also be within my power to do $\sim R$, even though it is logically necessary that I do R or $\sim R$. It may be within my power to stand and it may also be within my power not to stand, even though it is logically necessary that I do one or the other. Thus, $LN(R \vee \sim R)$ does not imply $PN(R) \vee PN(\sim R)$.

To return to the original question, assume that $LN(R \vee \sim R)$, i.e. it is logically necessary that I will do R or $\sim R$. Does this imply $T(R) \vee T(\sim R)$, i.e. that I will do R, or if I will not do R, then I will do $\sim R$? If this does follow, then $T(R) \vee T(\sim R)$ cannot imply anything which is not implied

17. Physical necessity is here used in the sense in which oxygen is necessary for human life, though oxygen is not logically necessary for human life.

by $LN(R \lor \sim R)$, since the latter logically implies the former.[18]

What is implied by the fact that I will do R, or if I will not do R, then I will do $\sim R$ has been clearly demonstrated in the proofs of fatalism discussed in the previous chapters. If it is true that I will do R, then nothing can occur which is sufficient for the nonoccurrence of R, i.e. R is necessary in the sense that nothing anyone can do can prevent R (I shall symbolize this sense of necessity as "F-necessity" or "FN," since it is this sense of necessity which is relevant to the question of fatalism, i.e. if all events are F-necessary, then fatalism is true). If it is true that I will do $\sim R$, then nothing can occur which is sufficient for the nonoccurrence of $\sim R$, i.e. $\sim R$ is F-necessary. Therefore, if it is true that R will occur, or if it is not true that R will occur, then $\sim R$ will occur, this implies that either it is not within anyone's power to prevent R or it is not within anyone's power to prevent $\sim R$, and that, therefore, either R is F-necessary or $\sim R$ is F-necessary.

Now what is implied by the fact that it is logically necessary that I will do either R or $\sim R$? Simply that it is not within anyone's power to prevent my doing either R or $\sim R$. What is not implied by the fact that it is logically necessary that I will do R or $\sim R$ is that either it is F-necessary that I will do R or that it is F-necessary that I will do $\sim R$. As we have seen, $LN(R \lor \sim R)$ does not imply $LN(R) \lor LN(\sim R)$. Similarly, $LN(R \lor \sim R)$ does not imply $PN(R) \lor PN(\sim R)$. Why should $LN(R \lor \sim R)$ imply $FN(R) \lor FN(\sim R)$? From the fact that it is logically necessary that an event will or will not occur, it does not follow that either its occurrence is logically necessary or that its nonoccurrence is logically necessary. Similarly, from the fact that it is logically necessary that an event will or will not occur, it does not follow that either its occurrence is physically

18. To put it simply, if A implies B, then A implies anything which B implies.

necessary or that its nonoccurrence is physically necessary. Therefore, it seems reasonable to assert that from the fact that it is logically necessary that an event will or will not occur, it does not follow that either its occurrence is F-necessary or that its nonoccurrence is F-necessary.

For example, assume that it is logically necessary that in five minutes I will be either standing or not standing. It may be within my power to be standing in five minutes and it may also be within my power not to be standing in five minutes. Thus, it may be neither F-necessary that I am standing in five minutes nor F-necessary that I am not standing in five minutes. Nevertheless, it is still logically necessary that in five minutes I will be either standing or not standing. Therefore, $LN(R \lor \sim R)$ does not imply $FN(R) \lor FN(\sim R)$. But, letting "T" stand for true, $LN(R \lor \sim R)$ does not then imply $T(R) \lor T(\sim R)$, since $T(R) \lor T(\sim R)$ implies that $FN(R) \lor FN(\sim R)$, whereas $LN(R \lor \sim R)$ is consistent with $\sim FN(R)$ and $\sim FN(\sim R)$. In other words, the fact that it is logically necessary that R or $\sim R$ does not imply that it is true that R, or if it is not true that R, then it is true that $\sim R$, for whereas the latter implies that either R is F-necessary or that $\sim R$ is F-necessary, the former is consistent with it being not F-necessary that R and also not F-necessary that $\sim R$.[19]

Now what consequences does this have for the onto-logical view of the laws of thought and for the pragmatic view of the laws of thought? Those who hold the ontological view can maintain that whereas it is logically necessary that every proposition is either true or false, it is not true that every proposition must be either true, or if not true, then false. Therefore, they are not committed to fatalism. They

19. Note that the foregoing discussion does not imply that $T(R) \lor T(\sim R)$ is not true for every action What the discussion does imply is that whether $T(R) \lor T(\sim R)$ is true for every action does not depend on the fact that $LN(R \lor \sim R)$ is true for every action.

can maintain that, whereas the fact that any proposition is necessarily either true or false reflects an ontological truth and therefore a logical requirement, the fact that any proposition must be either true, or if not true, then false, is false, since it does not reflect the basic structure of the world and could be falsified by a certain occurrence, viz. a future contingent event.

Those who hold the pragmatic view, however, are in somewhat more difficulty. The proponents of this view can assert that they do not hold that every proposition must be either true, or if not true, then false, but rather that every proposition must be either true or false. But why have they rejected the assertion that every proposition must be either true, or if not true, then false? They have not rejected it in order to achieve greater precision in language. They have rejected it in order to avoid the fatalistic implications of what at first appears to be purely a law of logic. It seems clear then that certain choices as to what should be laws of logic can have rather dire consequences. It might still be maintained by proponents of the pragmatic view that the statement that any proposition must be either true or false tells us nothing about the world and is merely a linguistic convention adopted to facilitate clarity in communication. This may be so, but what proponents of the pragmatic view must keep in mind is that it is not enough to assert, as Lewis does, that in adopting laws of thought "I am coerced only by my own need to understand."[20] Clearly, one is also coerced by the unfortunate implications of certain formulations of the laws of thought, which are not always free of ontological commitments.

What are the consequences of the above discussion for the truth or falsity of fatalism? It appeared at first that to maintain the law of excluded middle would logically commit one to fatalism. Now, however, we see that this need not be

20. Lewis, p. 291.

so if the law of excluded middle is interpreted in a certain way. If one maintains formulation (2) of the law of excluded middle, i.e. every proposition must be either true, or if not true, then false, then he is maintaining a proposition which commits him to fatalism. If, however, one denies formulation (2) and maintains formulation (1), i.e. every proposition must be either true or false, then he is maintaining an analytic proposition which does not commit him to fatalism. Let us now see precisely how the denial of formulation (2) and the adoption of formulation (1) enables one to avoid the fatalistic conclusions of each of the specific proofs of fatalism which were discussed in the previous chapters.

Aristotle's first argument utilized the following first three premises:

(1) Every proposition must be either true, or if not true, then false.

(2) Assume that one man affirms today that an event of a given character, e.g. a sea-fight, will occur tomorrow and another denies this.

(3) The statement of the one man corresponds with reality and that of the other does not.

In order to avoid the fatalistic conclusions of this argument it is necessary to take issue first with step (1) and then with step (3). Step (1) was originally presented as the law of excluded middle. As such it appeared to be an analytic principle which was unexceptionable. It is clear now that this is not the case. On the contrary, step (1) is a *synthetic* proposition which would be shown to be false simply by the occurrence of a contingent event. If this synthetic proposition is assumed to be true, fatalism will follow, for as step (3) shows, if it is, in fact, true, or if not true, then false, that a sea-fight will occur tomorrow, then the statement of the one man does correspond with reality and that of the other does not, and, therefore, the proof is sound.

But if one holds that step (1) is false and that it would be acceptable only if phrased as "every proposition must be either true or false," then step (3) does not follow, for if the sea-fight is, in fact, contingent, then the statement that it will occur does not correspond with reality, and the statement that it will not does not correspond with reality. The statement which does correspond with reality is that it will or will not occur. To assume that step (3) does follow from the rephrased step (1) is to assume that the event in question is not contingent. But this is to beg the issue, for what was at issue was whether or not the sea-fight is contingent. If the sea-fight is contingent, it is true that it may occur and it is true that it may not occur. This is inconsistent with it being true that it will occur and inconsistent with it being true that it will not occur; however, this *is* consistent with it being necessarily true that it will or will not occur. In other words, the future must issue in one of two directions (since those two directions are the exclusive possibilities, i.e. a middle possibility is excluded), but it is not yet true that it will issue in one direction and it is also not yet true that it will issue in the other direction.

If one asks why the future must issue in one of the two directions, there are at least two possible replies. A proponent of the ontological view of the laws of thought could reply that the future must issue in one of two directions because that is how the world is constructed. This is clearly seen if one tries to find an exception to this principle. As Blanshard puts it, "That the desk I am writing on is either a desk or not may be admitted to be a most unhelpful truth and one in which nobody but a philosopher would take the slightest interest. Does it say something true, however? Try to deny it and see."[21]

On the other hand a proponent of the pragmatic view of the laws of thought would reply that the future must issue

21. Blanshard, p. 427.

in one of two directions because we have so organized our language that it is meaningless to speak otherwise. As Lewis puts it,

> the law of the excluded middle formulates our decision that whatever is not designated by a certain term shall be designated by its negative. It declares our purpose to make, for every term, a complete dichotomy of experience, instead—as we might choose—of classifying on the basis of a tripartite division into opposites (as black and white) and the middle ground between the two. Our rejection of such tripartite division represents only our penchant for simplicity.[22]

Aristotle's Argument II has the following second premise: (2) If "a thing is white now, it was true before to say that it would be white, so that of anything that has taken place it was always true to say 'it is' or 'it will be.' " But this is so only if we agree to Aristotle's first premise, which turns out once again to be the synthetic and questionable formulation of the law of excluded middle: every proposition must be either true, or if not true, then false. This premise is true of many propositions, but it has fatalistic implications if it is applied to all propositions, and this is what is done in step (2). If a thing is white now, that does not imply that at some past time t_1 it would be white now, or if was not white now, it would be nonwhite now, for it may have been contingent at t_1 whether the thing would be white now. In such a case it is only correct at t_1 to say that either it will or will not be white now, and this does not imply that either it will be white now or it will not be white now. To assume that it does imply this is to beg the issue, for what was at issue was whether or not the thing's being white now is contingent, and it cannot be contingent at t_1 if it was true

22. Lewis, p. 287.

that it would be white now or if it was true that it would not be white now.

The fourth premise of Arthur Prior's reconstruction of Diodorus' Master Argument is: "if anything now neither is nor will be the case, then it has by now been the case that it will never be the case." But if we reject the synthetic formulation of the law of excluded middle, then if it is true now that an event e will not occur, it does not follow that it has by now been the case that e will not occur. If e was a contingent event until the present moment, then at any time prior to the present moment, we can truly say that e will or will not occur, but we cannot truly say that e will occur and we cannot truly say that e will never occur. Thus, Prior's fourth premise need not be accepted, and the fatalistic conclusion of his argument can be avoided without sacrificing the analytic law of excluded middle.

My proof of fatalism which is derived from certain theological considerations begins with this first step: "Every proposition must be either true, or if not true, then false." From this I deduce that at t_1 it is true, or if not true, then false, that I will perform R at t_2. I then assume that it is true at t_1 that I will perform R at t_2 and deduce from that the fact that it is fated that I will perform R at t_2. I assume then that it is false at t_1 that I will perform R at t_2, and I deduce from that the fact that it is fated that I will not perform R at t_2. Thus, in either case my action is fated. This whole line of argument, however, is dependent on the synthetic formulation of the law of excluded middle. If we substitute for step (1) step (1′), which reads "Every proposition must be either true or false," step (2) would then read "It is true or false that I will perform R at t_2." In that case the next step, it is either true that I will perform R at t_2 or else it is false that I will perform R at t_2, is a non sequitur, since this is not implied by step (1′). I can assume, as I do, that I will perform R at t_2 and I can assume, as I do, that I will not perform R at t_2, but it is not true that I will perform R at t_2 and it is also not true that I will not perform R at t_2. What is true is that necessarily I will or will not perform R at t_2, and this has no fatalistic implications.

Richard Taylor's proof rests on a similar error. He begins by assuming "the traditional law of excluded middle." He then states this law as "Every proposition is either true, or if not true, then false." In his first example he begins with the assertion that it is true, or if not true, then false, that a naval battle occurred yesterday. This is a very subtle move, since with regard to a proposition about the past, the two formulations of the law of excluded middle which we have discussed are extensionally equivalent. If it is true or false that a naval battle occurred yesterday, then it is also true, or if not true, then false, that a naval battle occurred yesterday. A past event is not contingent since we can do nothing now to prevent a past event from having happened. In the third step of his first example Taylor asserts "either P is true or P' is true." Since P is a past event, this is true on either interpretation of the law of excluded middle.

In his second example, which is formulated in a similar manner to the first, Taylor also employs a third step which reads: "either Q is true or Q' is true." Q here stands for a naval battle tomorrow. But this step is not quite parallel to that of the first example, since step (3) here might concern a contingent event. Therefore, it is incorrect to assume that if it is true that Q or Q', then it is true that Q or it is true that Q'. Of course, it is correct to assume that if it is true, or if not true, then false, that Q, then it is true that Q or it is true that Q' (which is equivalent to $\sim$Q). But, as we have seen, there is no reason to assume that it is true, or if not true, then false, that Q. All we need assume is that it is true that Q or Q', and this has no fatalistic implications. To assume the synthetic formulation of the law of excluded middle, as Taylor does, is to beg the issue, since the issue of whether or not Q is a contingent event reduces to the issue of whether the synthetic formulation of the law of excluded middle is applicable to it.

Thus, it appears that Aristotle, who formulated two proofs of fatalism, also provided a valid way of avoiding the conclusions of his own arguments. He points out that if a proposition affirms or denies, concerning a contingent event, that it will occur, that proposition is not true and it is not false, although any disjunction of one such proposition and its denial is necessarily true. In other words, Aristotle noted that although it is necessarily true that a contingent event will or will not occur, it is not yet true that it will occur and it is not yet false that it will occur; it may occur and it may not occur. Thus, although the future must issue in one of two directions, in the case of a contingent event it is not yet true that it will issue in one direction and it is not yet true that it will issue in the other direction. In this way Aristotle's position allows one logically to maintain both the law of excluded middle and man's free will. Far from such a position being, as Linsky argues, "absurd," it is exceptionally profound and provides a solution to the problem of fatalism.

8 Fate, Logic, and Time

Fatalism, as I originally defined it, is the thesis that the laws of logic alone suffice to prove that no man has free will. I have now examined all of the most important proofs of fatalism and have found them to be unsuccessful. This is not at all a surprising conclusion, since there are few, if any, philosophers today who believe that fatalism is true. What is surprising, however, is that the reasons generally advanced to demonstrate that fatalism is erroneous are themselves erroneous.

I have argued that, contrary to the almost unanimous opinion of contemporary philosophers, if one accepts the law of excluded middle in what I have termed its "synthetic" formulation, viz. every proposition must be either true, or if not true, then false, then he is thereby logically committed to deny man's free will. This has been demonstrated, I believe, by two proofs of Aristotle, Arthur Prior's reconstruction of Diodorus Cronus' Master Argument, my proof derived from certain theological considerations, and Richard Taylor's proof. These proofs have all been rejected by most contemporary philosophers on the ground that the premises which the proofs employ do not logically imply the denial of man's free will. It is my contention, however, that these rejected proofs *are* logically sound, and that their premises *do,* in fact, imply the denial of man's free will.

Nevertheless, it does not seem to me that any of these proofs actually show fatalism to be true. Each of these proofs fails, because each employs as a premise the synthetic law of excluded middle. This law, though it has been generally accepted as a law of logic is, in fact, an empirical generalization open to serious question. It is not, as those who hold the pragmatic view of the laws of thought would have us believe, a "minimal condition for discourse." Discourse without the synthetic law of excluded middle is just as intelligible as discourse with the synthetic law of excluded middle. Furthermore, the synthetic law of excluded middle is not, as those who hold the ontological view would have us believe, an incontrovertible and indisputable fact about the world. Quite to the contrary, the synthetic law of excluded middle would be shown to be false by the occurrence of a single action which a man had within his power both to perform and not to perform, and whether such actions have occurred or will occur has been a source of dispute for centuries.

This is not to say that the synthetic law of excluded middle is false. It may, in fact, be true, and if it is true and if it is considered as a law of logic, then fatalism is true, for, as we have seen, the synthetic law of excluded middle does logically imply that no man has free will.

But to prove fatalism in this way is to deprive it of its plausibility. In the first chapter I noted that there have been many nonfatalistic arguments designed to prove that no man has free will. All of these arguments, however, were open to the charge that their premises were no more plausible than was the denial of their conclusions, and that, therefore, the arguments themselves could be reasonably denied. For instance, it has been argued that since every event has a cause, no man has free will. This argument, however, is open to the charge that it is just as plausible to assert that man has free will as to assert that every event has a cause. Thus, since the premise of the argument is no more plausible than the denial of the conclusion, the argument itself can be reasonably denied.

This difficulty, though, is avoided by fatalistic arguments, since the premises which these arguments utilize are the

laws of logic which no rational man wishes to deny. Therefore, if it could be shown that *these* laws imply that no man
has free will, the proof would be strong indeed, for to deny
it would be to deny logic itself.

If one employs the synthetic law of excluded middle to
prove that no man has free will and then claims that this
law is a law of logic, I believe he is on doubtful grounds.
This so-called "law of logic" is merely an empirical generalization which is no more plausible than the claim that man
has free will. Therefore, this proof is no more convincing
than are many other proofs designed to prove that no man
has free will. These other proofs may use as premises such
theses as these: every event has a cause; every man must
do what he believes to be best; a man's conscious decisions
are always controlled by unconscious factors over which
he has no control. It is not that one or all of these theses may
not be true. They do not, however, suffice as premises in
an argument designed to prove that no man has free will,
for they are no more plausible than the assertion that man
does have free will. The synthetic law of excluded middle,
utilized as a premise in a proof designed to show that no
man has free will, suffers from the same weakness.

If one rejects the synthetic law of excluded middle as it
applies to certain statements concerning future contingent
events and, thereby, avoids a logical commitment to deny
man's free will, is he, thereby, logically committed to deny
the analytic law of excluded middle? The analytic law of
excluded middle, any proposition must be either true or
false, is not implied by the synthetic law of excluded middle.
As I pointed out in the previous chapter, $LN(P \vee \sim P)$
does not imply $T(P) \vee T(\sim P)$, i.e. the logical necessity of
$(P \vee \sim P)$ does not imply that P is true, or if P is not true,
then $\sim P$ is true. Therefore, one can maintain the analytic
law of excluded middle while rejecting the synthetic law of
excluded middle.

Maintaining the analytic law of excluded middle, however, does not commit one to deny man's free will. But if one rejects the synthetic law of excluded middle, is there any reason to maintain the analytic law of excluded middle?

The analytic law of excluded middle, unlike the synthetic law of excluded middle, does appear to be an incontrovertible truth. To affirm that an event did or did not occur, that an event is or is not occurring, that an event will or will not occur, does seem to be affirming what is incontrovertibly so. It is the analytic law of excluded middle which embodies what has been traditionally known as a "law of thought." According to the pragmatic view of the laws of thought, the analytic law of excluded middle is a necessary condition for intelligible discourse. According to the ontological view, the analytic law of excluded middle reflects an incontrovertible fact about the world. According to either of these views, however, the analytic law of excluded middle is a principle which is surely true. Consider, for instance, a man who "risks" his money by betting that a certain horse will or will not win a certain race. He is not betting that the horse will win the race. He is not betting that the horse will not win the race. What he is betting is that the horse will or will not win the race. Such a bet is surely no risk at all, for nothing could be more certain than that the horse will or will not win the race.

Thus, if one wishes to avoid fatalism and yet not violate reason itself, one must reject, as Aristotle did, the synthetic law of excluded middle and accept, as he did, the analytic law of excluded middle.[1] However, the decision to adopt

1. Aristotle rejected the synthetic law of excluded middle both as a logical principle and as an empirical fact. However, in order to avoid fatalism one need only reject it as a logical principle. But to reject it as a logical principle one must also reject certain generally accepted views which will be discussed in the remainder of this chapter.

Aristotle's solution to the problem of fatalism is far from the end of the matter, for this decision has many important and controversial implications.[2]

We have seen that in order to avoid fatalism, one must hold that any proposition which affirms or denies, concerning a contingent event, that it will occur is not true, though it is not false. Nevertheless, to maintain the analytic law of excluded middle, one must hold that any disjunction of such a proposition and its denial is necessarily true. For example, let P represent a proposition which affirms that a contingent event will occur. In order to avoid fatalistic implications, one must hold that (1) P is not true, (2) P is not false, (3) $\sim P$ (the contradictory of P) is not true, and (4) $\sim P$ is not false. In order to maintain the analytic law of excluded middle, one must hold that $(P \vee \sim P)$ is necessarily true, i.e. true by virtue of logic alone.

Traditional logic utilized only two truth-values. It maintained that if a proposition was not true, it must be false; and if it was not false, it must be true. The denial of the synthetic law of excluded middle with regard to certain statements concerning future contingent events would, however, seem to entail an exception to this two-valued logic, for it implies that there are certain propositions which are not true, though they also are not false. Such propositions affirm or deny, concerning a contingent event, that it will occur. Such propositions require a third truth-value.

Modern logicians have developed what is known as a three-valued logic. Such a logic provides for the case in which a proposition is not true and not false, by providing a third truth-value which such a proposition may possess. The best-known system of three-valued logic was created by the Polish logician Jan Lukasiewicz, who created his three-valued logic specifically for the purpose of providing a logi-

2. A penetrating discussion of this aspect of the problem is to be found in Ronald J. Butler's "Aristotle's Sea Fight and Three-Valued Logic," *The Philosophical Review.* 64 (1955), 264–74.

cal framework for Aristotle's doctrine of future contingencies.[3] This system was further developed by A. N. Prior, who also envisioned it as a logical tool for dealing with the problem of future contingencies.[4]

To see how such a three-valued logic works,[5] let us consider a proposition, represented by P, which affirms that a contingent event e will occur. According to three-valued logic, P is not true and P is not false. It is, rather, indeterminate.[6] If P is indeterminate, then $\sim P$ is also indeterminate, for if the occurrence of e is contingent, then so is the nonoccurrence of e.

It should be noted that three-valued logic does not imply an exception to the law of contradiction. That law states that if a proposition is true, then its contradictory must be false, and if a proposition is false, then its contradictory must be true.[7] According to three-valued logic, if P is true, then $\sim P$ is false. Similarly, if $\sim P$ is true, then P is false. If P is indeterminate, then $\sim P$ is indeterminate. Thus, three-valued

3. The system and its relation to Aristotle's views can be found in Jan Lukasiewicz, "Philosophische Bemerkungen zu mehrwertigen Systemen des Aussagenkalkuls," *Comptes Rendus des Séances de la Société des Sciences et des Lettres de Varsovie* (*Sprawozdania z pozesieden Towarzystwa Naukowego Warszawskiego*), Classe III, Vol. XXIII (1930), Fascicule 1–3, pp. 51–77. One of the key passages is translated in Baylis, p. 159.

4. Arthur Prior, *Formal Logic* (Oxford, 1962), pt. III, no. II.

5. It should be noted that in order to avoid the fatalistic conclusions of the arguments presented in Chapters 3, 4, 5, and 6 it is not necessary to adopt any one particular system of three-valued logic. What I am proposing is the adoption of a third truth-value, and this is consistent with the adoption of any one of many three-valued logical systems. One such system is suggested in Storrs McCall's perceptive article, "Temporal Flux," *American Philosophical Quarterly, 3* (1966), 270–81.

6. Prior uses the term "neuter." I prefer the more descriptive term "indeterminate."

7. For a discussion of the notion of a "contradictory," see Chapter 4.

logic in no sense constitutes an exception to the law of contradiction.

But does three-valued logic entail an exception to the law
of excluded middle? C. I. Lewis and C. H. Langford, in
their discussion of Lukasiewicz' system of three-valued
logic, note that such a logic "requires that the Law of Excluded Middle, 'Every proposition is either true or false,'
must be repudiated as a false principle."[8]

Here again it is necessary to distinguish between the
synthetic law of excluded middle and the analytic law of
excluded middle. According to the synthetic law of excluded
middle, every proposition must be either true, or if not true,
then false, i.e. for any interpretation of P, "P" is true or
"$\sim P$" is true. Three-valued logic does imply an exception to
this law, for according to three-valued logic there are propositions which are *not* true and *not* false. Consider the
proposition represented by P which affirms that a contingent event will occur. It is not the case that P is true, and it
is not the case that P is false. Thus, it is not the case that P
is either true, or if not true, then false, and the synthetic law
of excluded middle is thereby repudiated.

But does a proposition which is not true and not false
constitute an exception to the analytic law of excluded
middle? That law states that every proposition is either true
or false, i.e. for any interpretation of P, "P or $\sim P$" is true.
Consider again the proposition represented by P which affirms that a contingent event e will occur. P is *not* true. P is
not false. But "P or $\sim P$" is true, in the sense that e will or
will not occur, though it is not true that e will occur and it is
not true that e will not occur.

This does not imply, however, that either e will occur,
or if e will not occur, then $\sim e$ (the nonoccurrence of e)
will occur. The analytic law of excluded middle does not
state either that P is true or that P is false, i.e. e will occur

8. Clarence Irving Lewis and Cooper Harold Langford, *Symbolic Logic* (New York, 1959), p. 222.

or e will not occur. What it does state is that P is either true or false, i.e. e will or will not occur. In other words, the analytic law of excluded middle is a limiting but not a determining principle. It limits the possibilities to the occurrence and nonoccurrence of e, but neither determines that e will occur, nor determines that e will not occur. The analytic law of excluded middle implies only that one of two possibilities will occur; it does not imply that one possibility will occur, nor does it imply that the other possibility will occur. To put this in terms of the symbolism I utilized in the previous chapter, the analytic law of excluded middle, $LN(P \vee \sim P)$, implies that $T(P \vee \sim P)$, but just as $LN(P \vee \sim P)$ does not imply $LN(P) \vee LN(\sim P)$, so $T(P \vee \sim P)$ does not imply that $T(P) \vee T(\sim P)$.

It is thus possible to maintain the analytic law of excluded middle while admitting that a specific proposition is not true and not false. But if it is not true and if it is not false, it must have some other truth-value. Three-valued logic provides such a truth-value.

In order to see clearly just why the introduction of a third truth-value is necessary to avoid fatalism, consider Aristotle's example of a sea-fight tomorrow. If one affirms that a sea-fight will occur tomorrow, then he is, as we have seen, logically committed to the view that no one can prevent the occurrence of a sea-fight tomorrow; if one affirms that a sea-fight will not occur tomorrow, then he is logically committed to the view that no one can bring about the occurrence of a sea-fight tomorrow. But if it is not true that a sea-fight will occur tomorrow, and if it is also not false that a sea-fight will occur tomorrow, what truth-value does the proposition "there will be a sea-fight tomorrow" have? It must have a truth-value to be meaningful, and it certainly is a meaningful proposition.[9] It implies that the present situation is com-

9. It might be argued that "there will be a sea-fight tomorrow" is not a proposition at all, but rather a prediction, proposal, promise,

patible with someone bringing about the occurrence of a sea-fight tomorrow and the present situation is also compatible with someone preventing the occurrence of a sea-fight tomorrow, and empirical evidence is certainly relevant to verifying or disconfirming this description of the present situation. For instance, if all ships on both sides of a war have been sunk, that would constitute strong evidence against anyone's having it within his power to bring about a sea-fight tomorrow. Thus, the proposition "there will be a sea-fight tomorrow" is clearly meaningful. But if a proposition is to be meaningful, it must have a truth-value. If it is not true and it is not false, it must have a third truth-value, and it is such a truth-value which three-valued logic provides.

Aristotle's solution to the problem of fatalism thus implies a three-valued logic. But, Aristotle's solution has other consequences which are equally as important and equally as controversial, if not more controversial, than a three-valued logic. These consequences strike at the heart of certain generally accepted views of the nature of propositions as well as the nature of time.

Most modern logic utilizes only propositions which do not change their truth-value from one time to another. If a proposition is true, it has always been true and will always

---

etc. I see no reason to adopt such an approach, however, since it offers no real advantages while creating unnecessary difficulties. For example, if the sea-fight is necessary (whether or not the speaker knows it) the speaker is predicting, proposing, etc. If the sea-fight is not necessary, the speaker is uttering a proposition. This would be most peculiar, since I should think that whether a man is predicting or proposing or promising depends to a great extent on his intention and not on the contingency of a future event, a contingency of which he may be totally unaware. In addition, this approach would have the odd consequence of denying that "there will be a sea-fight tomorrow" is a proposition, while affirming that "there was a sea-fight yesterday" *is* a proposition.

be true. If a proposition is false, it has always been false and will always be false. As Quine puts it:

> Logical analysis is facilitated by requiring rather that each *statement* be true once and for all or false once and for all, independently of time. This can be effected by rendering verbs tenseless and then resorting to explicit chronological descriptions when need arises for distinctions of time. The sentence, "The Nazis will annex Bohemia," uttered as true on May 9, 1936, corresponds to the statement, "The Nazis annex [tenseless] Bohemia after May 9, 1936"; and this statement is true once and for all, regardless of date of utterance.[10]

Quine is hardly alone in this opinion. His position has been supported by Bertrand Russell,[11] Ayer,[12] and J. N. Findlay, the last declaring that "if we avoided the adverbs 'here' and 'there,' if we purged our language of tenses, and talked exclusively in terms of dates and tenseless participles, we should never be involved in difficulties."[13]

However, as I pointed out in Chapter 3, the program advocated by Quine and those who agree with him that attempts to render all propositions tenseless without altering their meaning is doomed to failure. A proposition's tense may be shifted from the verb to an adverbial phrase, but the tense cannot be altogether eliminated without altering the meaning of the proposition. A proposition's tense is thus an integral and uneliminable part of the proposition.

This may seem to be an uninteresting logical point, but,

10. W. V. O. Quine, *Elementary Logic* (New York, 1965), p 6.

11. Bertrand Russell, *An Inquiry into Meaning and Truth* (London, 1940), p. 113.

12. A. J. Ayer, *Philosophical Essays* (London, 1963), p. 186.

13. J. N. Findlay, "Time: A Treatment of Some Puzzles," in Anthony Flew, ed., *Logic and Language*, p. 58.

in fact, it has serious repercussions for fatalism. Aristotle's solution to the problem of fatalism depends on a proposition's tense being an uneliminable part of the proposition, for Aristotle's solution implies that a proposition can have two different truth-values, depending on the tense of the proposition. If Quine's view were correct, a proposition's tense could have no effect on the proposition's truth-value, for the tense would be, in principle, eliminable. Therefore, Aristotle's solution to the problem of fatalism would be impossible and, as we have seen, Aristotle's solution is the only way of avoiding fatalism while still preserving logic.

In order to see just why Aristotle's solution to the problem of fatalism depends upon a proposition's changing its truth-value,[14] consider a proposition, represented by P, which affirms that a sea-fight occurs on September 7, 1948 ("occurs" to be understood tenselessly). If it was true on Sept. 6, 1948, that a sea-fight would occur on Sept. 7, 1948, then, as we have seen, it was fated on Sept. 6 that a sea-fight would occur on Sept. 7.[15] If it was true on Sept. 6 that a sea-fight would not take place on Sept. 7, then it was fated on Sept. 6 that a sea-fight would not take place on Sept. 7. But, if neither the occurrence of a sea-fight on Sept. 7 nor the non-occurrence of a sea-fight on Sept. 7 was fated on Sept. 6, then it was not true and it was not false on Sept. 6 that a sea-fight would occur on Sept. 7. But the proposition "a sea-fight occurs on Sept. 7, 1948" must have had a truth-value on Sept. 6. This is the truth-value which I have chosen to call "indeterminate."

14. In other words it was not within anyone's power to prevent a sea-fight on Sept. 7.

15. It seems to me that regardless of my previous analysis, anyone committed to man's free will is committed to a proposition being able to change its truth-value. For example, if it is true that I will do A at t_1, then the proposition "I will do A at t_1" is true. If I can refrain from A at t_1, then I can render the proposition "I will do A at t_1" false, and thus I can change its truth-value, even if I don't exercise that option.

But, on Sept. 8, 1948, the proposition "a sea-fight occurs on Sept. 7, 1948" must be either true, or if not true, then false, for if it were indeterminate on Sept. 8 whether a sea-fight occurred on Sept. 7, it would be within a man's power on Sept. 8 to prevent a sea-fight on Sept. 7 and it would also be within a man's power on Sept. 8 to bring about a sea-fight on Sept. 7, and this is absurd. Therefore, if it is not fated on Sept. 6 that a sea-fight will occur on Sept. 7, the proposition "a sea-fight occurs on Sept. 7, 1948" is indeterminate on Sept. 6 and either true, or if not true, then false on Sept. 8. In either case the proposition changes its truth-value from Sept. 6 to Sept. 8.

Thus, if one is to avoid fatalism and preserve logic, a proposition's truth-value must be subject to change. Indeed, this is not all a proposition must be able to change. A proposition's modality must also be subject to change. This is another idea which is unacceptable to many modern logicians. For instance, Donald Williams writes as follows:

> Even if we adopt the debatable maxim that the more absurd an idea is, the less likely it is to have been espoused by Aristotle, the idea which I impute would have to go far to vie with what Mr. Linsky imputes, viz., that the modality of a proposition, instead of depending on its logical form or other intrinsic character, depends on the *date,* so that exactly the same proposition which at 11:59 A.M. is contingent, at noon is necessary.[16]

It is important to note, however, that a proposition can have more than one kind of modality. Aristotle's solution to the problem of fatalism does *not* imply that a proposition which is logically contingent (i.e. a synthetic proposition) at one time may be logically necessary (i.e. an analytic proposition) at another time.

16. Donald Williams, "Professor Linsky on Aristotle," *The Philosophical Review, 63* (1954), 255.

The term "necessary" as used in the context of the issue
of fatalism has the following meaning: an event is necessary
if no man has it within his power to prevent the occurrence
of the event; similarly, a proposition is necessary if no man
has it within his power to falsify the proposition.

The term "contingent" as used in the context of the issue
of fatalism has a similar meaning: an event is contingent
if it is not the case that the occurrence of the event is necessary and if it is not the case that the nonoccurrence of the
event is necessary (i.e. if a man has it within his power to
prevent the occurrence of the event, and if a man has it
within his power to bring about the occurrence of the event);
a proposition is contingent if it is not the case that the
proposition is necessary and if it is not the case that the
contradictory of the proposition is necessary (i.e. if a man
can falsify the proposition, and if a man can falsify the contradictory of the proposition). Thus, what Aristotle's solution to the problem of fatalism does imply is that a proposition may be falsifiable at one time and not falsifiable at
another time.

In order to see clearly just why Aristotle's solution does
imply that a proposition's modality must be subject to
change, consider again the proposition (P) "A sea-fight occurs on Sept. 7, 1948" ("occurs" to be considered tenselessly). If it was true on Sept. 6 that a sea-fight would occur
on Sept. 7, then as we have seen, no man could on Sept. 6
prevent the occurrence of a sea-fight on Sept. 7, and it would
not be within any man's power on Sept. 6 to falsify P. If it
was true on Sept. 6 that a sea-fight would not take place on
Sept. 7, then, as we have seen, no man could on Sept. 6
bring about the occurrence of a sea-fight on Sept. 7, and
it would not be within anyone's power on Sept. 6 to render
P true. Thus, whether P is true on Sept. 6 or whether P is
false on Sept. 6, either the occurrence of a sea-fight on Sept.
7 is fated on Sept. 6 or the nonoccurrence of a sea-fight on
Sept. 7 is fated on Sept. 6.

Neither one is fated on Sept. 6 *only* if on Sept. 6 P is not true and P is not false, but P is indeterminate. If it is indeterminate on Sept. 6 whether a sea-fight will occur on Sept. 7, then it is within some man's power on Sept. 6 to bring about the occurrence of a sea-fight on Sept. 7, and it is also within some man's power on Sept. 6 to prevent a sea-fight on Sept. 7. Thus, if it is indeterminate on Sept. 6 whether a sea-fight will occur on Sept. 7, P, as well as ~P, is a contingent proposition on Sept. 6, for on Sept. 6 it is within some man's power to falsify P and it is also within some man's power to render P true. Thus, if a sea-fight on Sept. 7 is not fated on Sept. 6, P is a contingent proposition on Sept. 6.

As we have seen before, however, it is not up to anyone on Sept. 8 whether or not a sea-fight occurred on Sept. 7, for if this were the case, it would be within a man's power on Sept. 8 to prevent a sea-fight on Sept. 7, and it would also be within a man's power on Sept. 8 to bring about a sea-fight on Sept. 7, and this is absurd. Therefore, on Sept. 8 either P is necessary or ~P is necessary.

So, if it is not fated on Sept. 6 that a sea-fight will occur on Sept. 7, the proposition (P) "A sea-fight occurs on Sept. 7, 1948" is contingent on Sept. 6 as is the proposition (~P) "A sea-fight does not occur on Sept. 7, 1948." But, on Sept. 8 either P is necessary or ~P is necessary.[17] In either case a proposition has changed its modality. Indeed, both P and ~P have changed their modality, for whichever proposition is necessary, the other proposition is impossible, i.e. it is not within any man's power to render the proposition true. For instance, if a sea-fight actually occurred on Sept. 7, then on Sept. 8 the proposition P is necessary and the proposition ~P is impossible, for on Sept. 8 no man can falsify P and no man can render ~P true. Thus, if one is to avoid fatalism

17. "Necessary," of course, in the sense that no one can prevent its occurrence.

and preserve logic, a proposition's modality must be subject to change.

These possible changes in a proposition's truth-value and modality are not merely logical peculiarities. The possibility of such changes is logically incompatible with at least two commonly held metaphysical theories of the nature of time.

The first of these theories is expressed by Bertrand Russell:

> There is some sense, easier to feel than to state, in which time is an unimportant and superficial characteristic of reality. Past and future must be acknowledged to be as real as the present, and a certain emancipation from slavery to time is essential to philosophic thought.[18]

This "emancipation from slavery to time" was so eloquently expressed by Spinoza:

> Things are conceived by us as actual in two ways— either in so far as we conceive them to exist with relation to a fixed time and place or in so far as we conceive them to be contained in God and to follow from the necessity of the divine nature. But those things which are conceived in this second way as true or real we conceive under the form of eternity, and their ideas involve the eternal and infinite essence of God.[19]

This same idea of time as a mere "superficial" aspect of reality underlies the metaphysical position defended by Donald Williams:

> I do wish to defend the view of the world, or the manner of speaking about it, which treats the totality

18. Bertrand Russell, *Our Knowledge of the External World* (London, 1929), p. 171.

19. Benedict De Spinoza, *Ethics,* ed. James Gutmann (New York, 1957), Part Five, Proposition XXIX, Note.

> of being, of facts, or of events, as spread out eternally
> in the dimension of time as well as the dimensions of
> space . . . there "exists" an eternal world total in which
> past and future events are as determinately located,
> characterized, and truly describable as are southern
> events and western events.[20]

Williams does not specifically state that time is unimportant
or "superficial," but his position obviously implies that the
future is just as real as the past, and that time is of no importance in evaluating what are "facts" and what are not
"facts."

A similar metaphysical thesis lies at the heart of Quine's
program to require "that each statement be true once and
for all or false once and for all, independently of time."
Indeed, Quine utilizes the term "eternal sentence" to refer
to a sentence "whose truth-value stays fixed through time
and from speaker to speaker," and he argues that any sentence can be transformed without loss of meaning to an
"eternal sentence."[21]

This metaphysical thesis, however, is logically incompatible with the possibility of a proposition changing its
truth-value or modality depending upon the time at which
it is stated, and, as we have seen, it is just such a possibility
which provides the only logical escape from fatalism. If time
is but a "superficial" aspect of reality, if a true proposition
must be eternally true, if the "facts" are "spread out eternally," then the time at which a proposition is stated has no
relevance to its truth-value or modality.

Note that I am not here referring to propositions which
are incomplete due to a lack of specification of time, place,
or person. "It is raining," "I am swimming," or "Jones is
running" are incomplete propositions whose truth-value or

20. Williams, "The Sea Fight Tomorrow," pp. 282, 305–06.
21. Quine, *Word and Object* (Cambridge, Mass., 1960), p. 193.

modality can change without in any way casting doubt upon the metaphysical theory which declares time to be a "superficial" aspect of reality. For instance, "It is raining" may be true in New York, but false in Boston. It may be true at noon, but false at midnight. "I am swimming" may be true of one person, but false of another. "Jones is running" is necessary when Jones is running, but impossible when Jones is dead.

However, it is not such incomplete propositions to which I am referring when I argue that the possibility of a proposition's truth-value or modality being subject to change is logically incompatible with the metaphysical theory of the superficiality of time. I am referring, rather, to propositions such as "George Washington is crossing the Delaware River at 12:00 A.M. on December 25, 1776" ("is crossing" to be considered tenselessly), which are complete as to time, place, and person. If we are to preserve logic and avoid fatalism, such a proposition's truth-value and modality must be subject to change. However, according to the view of time propounded by Russell, Williams, Quine, and others, such a change is impossible, for the "facts" are all there already, the "facts" are "eternal," and time is a "superficial" aspect of reality which does not affect these "eternal facts." Thus, this view of time, which Williams confidently refers to as a "truism,"[22] is logically incompatible with man's free will. If this view of time is a truism, then so is fatalism.

There is a second commonly held theory of time which is logically incompatible with the possibility of a proposition's truth-value or modality being subject to change. This theory does not claim that time is a superficial aspect of reality. It claims that time is no aspect of reality, for time is not real.

The view that time is unreal has a long and distinguished history in philosophic thought. One of the first philosophers

22. Williams, p. 282.

to argue formally for this thesis was St. Augustine.[23] He argued that "if the present were always present and never flowed into the past, it would not be time at all, but eternity."[24] Since, according to St. Augustine, the "past" must be identified with memory and the "future" with expectation, and since memory and expectation are both present facts, all "time" is present, and thus is not time, but eternity. What are usually identified as past, present, and future should, according to St. Augustine, be properly identified as "a present of things past, a present of things present, a present of things future."[25]

A similar view of time was expressed by Immanuel Kant in his *Critique of Pure Reason*. He argued that "time [is] merely the subjective condition under which all our intuitions take place."[26] F. H. Bradley, expressing a similar view, referred to time as "illusory,"[27] and J. M. E. McTaggert likewise referred to time as a mere "appearance."[28]

This is an even more extreme metaphysical view than that supported by Russell, Williams, and Quine. Russell, though he considers time to be a "superficial" aspect of reality, does admit that "past and future must be acknowledged to be as real as the present." But though the view of time espoused by St. Augustine, Kant, Bradley, and others is

23. It is not my purpose here to discuss the philosophy of St. Augustine or of any other thinker whose views I quote subsequently. I am only alluding to them to show some implications of Aristotle's thesis concerning future contingencies.

24. St. Augustine, *The Confessions of St. Augustine,* trans. F. J. Sheed (New York, 1943), Book Eleven, section XIV, p. 271.

25. Ibid., Book Eleven, section XX, p. 276.

26. Immanuel Kant, *Critique of Pure Reason,* trans. J. M. D. Meiklejohn (New York, 1901), p. 73.

27. F. H. Bradley, *Appearance and Reality* (Oxford, 1959), p. 183.

28. J. M. E. McTaggert, "The Unreality of Time," in *Philosophical Studies* (London, 1934), p. 131.

contrary to that of Russell, it is, as is Russell's view, logically incompatible with Aristotle's solution to the problem of fatalism.

As we have seen, Aristotle's solution requires that a proposition's truth-value and modality depend upon the time at which the proposition is stated. According to Aristotle's solution, a proposition may be indeterminate at one time and true, or if not true, then false at another time. Similarly, according to Aristotle's solution, a proposition may be contingent at one time and either necessary, or if not necessary, then impossible at another time. But if time is unreal, then it cannot affect a proposition's truth-value or modality, and if time cannot affect a proposition's truth-value or modality, we must either accept fatalism or reject logic.

Aristotle's solution to the problem of fatalism thus has at least three metaphysical implications concerning the nature of time. First, time is real. According to Aristotle's solution, the truth-value and modality of a proposition depend upon the time at which the proposition is stated. If time is not real, it could not affect the truth-value or modality of a proposition, and Aristotle's solution would be erroneous.

Second, time is "efficacious," i.e. time alone can affect a man's powers or abilities.[29] According to Aristotle's solution, certain events in the future are contingent, whereas all events in the past are, by virtue of their pastness alone, necessary, i.e. it is not within any man's power to prevent their occurrence. Thus, future possibilities, which are at one time within a man's power to realize and also within his power not to realize, cease to be possibilities due to the mere lapse of time. Time alone thus can decrease a man's powers or abilities. If time were not efficacious, Aristotle's solution would be erroneous, for either all future events would be necessary, or else some past events would be contingent.

29. The term "efficacious" is suggested in Richard Taylor's *Metaphysics*, p. 58.

Third, time has an intrinsic sense of asymmetry. According to Aristotle's solution, the future differs from the past, and not merely in the sense that it comes later. Possibilities exist in the future in a sense in which no possibilities exist in the past. I can exert some measure of control over what will happen in the future, whereas I can exert no such control over what has happened in the past. This is commonly expressed by saying that the past is "closed," while the future is, in part, "open." If this were not the case, Aristotle's solution would be erroneous.

C. D. Broad once wrote that philosophy enables us "to replace a vague belief by a clear and analysed one, and a merely instinctive belief by one that has passed the fire of criticism."[30] Almost all men are firmly convinced that fatalism is false. However, in order to maintain this belief logically, and not merely instinctively, one must distinguish between two forms of the law of excluded middle.

What I have referred to as the synthetic law of excluded middle does logically imply that no man has free will. But to term the synthetic law of excluded middle a "law of logic" seems to me a distortion. The truth of the synthetic law of excluded middle can be decided only on empirical grounds, not on logical grounds. Fatalism, which depends for its plausibility on the fact that it utilizes premises which are indubitable and undeniable laws of logic, cannot be sustained by utilizing as a premise the synthetic law of excluded middle which is not a law of logic.

On the other hand, what I have referred to as the analytic law of excluded middle is an indubitable and undeniable law of logic. It does not, however, logically imply that no man has free will, and it does not, therefore, suffice to prove that fatalism is true.

30. C. D. Broad, *Scientific Thought* (Paterson, N.J., 1959), p. 15.

Thus, if one wishes to preserve logic and yet avoid fatalism, one must adopt the solution presented by Aristotle more than two thousand years ago, viz. rejecting the synthetic law of excluded middle, accepting the analytic law of excluded middle, and accepting all the meta-logical and meta-temporal implications of such a position.

Bibliography

Abelson, Raziel, "Taylor's Fatal Fallacy," *The Philosophical Review, 72* (1963), 93–96.

Albritton, Rogers, "Present Truth and Future Contingency," *The Philosophical Review, 66* (1957), 29–46.

Anscombe, G. E. M., "Aristotle and the Sea Battle," *Mind, 65* (1956), 1–15.

Anselm, St., *Proslogium,* trans. S. W. Deane, in *St. Anselm: Basic Writings,* La Salle, Illinois, Open Court, 1962.

Aquinas, St. Thomas, *Summa Theologica,* trans. Fathers of the English Dominican Province, London, Burns, Oates & Washington, Ltd., 1920.

Aristotle, *De Interpretatione,* trans. E. M. Edghill, in *The Basic Works of Aristotle,* ed. Richard McKeon, New York, Random House, 1941.

————, *Metaphysics,* trans. W. D. Ross, in *The Basic Works of Aristotle.*

Augustine, St., *The City of God,* trans. Marcus Dods, New York, The Modern Library, 1950.

————, *The Confessions of St. Augustine,* trans. F. J. Sheed, New York, Sheed & Ward, 1943.

————, *On Free Choice of the Will,* trans. Anna S. Benjamin and L. H. Hackstaff, New York, Library of Liberal Arts, 1964.

Aune, Bruce, "Fatalism and Professor Taylor," *The Philosophical Review, 71* (1962), 512–19.

Aureoli, Petrus, *I Sententiarum* (Rome, 1596), quoted in Frederick Copleston, *A History of Philosophy, 3.*

Ayer, A. J., *Language, Truth and Logic,* second ed. New York, Dover, 1946.

————, *The Problem of Knowledge,* London, Penguin Books, 1957.

———, "Statements About the Past," in *Philosophical Essays,* London, Macmillan & Co., 1963.

———, "Fatalism," in *The Concept Of A Person and other essays,* New York, St. Martin's Press, 1963.

———, ed., *Logical Positivism,* Glencoe, Illinois, The Free Press, 1959.

Baylis, Charles A., "Are Some Propositions Neither True Nor False?" *Philosophy of Science, 3* (1936), 156–66.

Blanshard, Brand, *Reason and Analysis,* London, Allen & Unwin, 1962.

Bochenski, I. M., *A History of Formal Logic,* Notre Dame, Indiana, Indiana University Press, 1961.

Boethius, *The Consolation of Philosophy,* trans. Richard Green, New York, Library of Liberal Arts, 1962.

Bradley, F. H., *Appearance and Reality,* Oxford, Clarendon Press, 1959.

Broad, C. D., *Scientific Thought,* Paterson, N.J., Littlefield, Adams & Co., 1959.

Brown, Charles D., "Fallacies in Taylor's 'Fatalism,'" *The Journal of Philosophy, 62* (1965), 349–53.

Butler, Ronald J., "Aristotle's Sea Fight and Three-Valued Logic," *The Philosophical Review, 64* (1955), 264–74.

Cahn, Steven, "Fatalistic Arguments," *The Journal of Philosophy, 61* (1964), 295–305.

Cicero, *De Fato,* trans. H. Rackham, Cambridge, Mass., Harvard University Press, 1960.

Cohen, Morris R., *Reason and Nature,* Glencoe, Illinois, The Free Press, 1953.

Copleston, Frederick, *A History of Philosophy, 1, 3,* Garden City, New York, Image Books, 1962.

Danto, Arthur, *Analytical Philosophy of History,* Cambridge, At the University Press, 1965.

Darrow, Clarence, *Attorney for the Damned,* ed. Arthur Weinberg, New York, Simon and Schuster, 1957.

Edwards, Jonathan, *Freedom of the Will,* ed. Paul Ramsey, New Haven, Yale University Press, 1957.

Epictetus, *Dissertationes ab Arriano Digestae,* ed. H. Schenkl, Leipzig, 1898, quoted in Kneale and Kneale, *The Development of Logic.*

Feigl, Herbert, and Brodbeck, May, eds., *Readings in the Philosophy of Science,* New York, Appleton-Century-Crofts, 1953.

Feigl, Herbert, and Sellars, Wilfrid, eds., *Readings in Philosophical Analysis,* New York, Appleton-Century-Crofts, 1949.

Findlay, J. N., "Time: A Treatment of Some Puzzles," in Anthony Flew, ed., *Logic and Language,* Garden City, Anchor Books, 1965.

Gale, Richard, "Is It Now Now?" *Mind, 73* (1964), 97–105.

Gersom, Levi ben, *The Commentary of Levi ben Gersom (Gersonides) on the Book of Job,* trans. Abraham L. Lassen, New York, Bloch Publishing Co., 1946.

Grünbaum, Adolf, "Causality and the Science of Human Behavior," in Herbert Feigl and May Brodbeck, eds., *Readings in the Philosophy of Science.*

Hartshorne, Charles, *Man's Vision of God,* New York, Willett, Clark & Co., 1941.

———, "Deliberation and Excluded Middle," *The Journal of Philosophy, 61* (1964), 476–77.

———, "The Meaning of 'Is going to be,'" *Mind, 74* (1965), 46–58.

Hegel, Georg Wilhelm Friedrich, *The Philosophy of History,* trans. J. Sibree, New York, Dover Publications, Inc., 1956.

Hintikka, Jaakko, "The Once and Future Sea Fight," *The Philosophical Review, 73* (1964), 461–92.

———, "Aristotle and the 'Master Argument' of Diodorus," *American Philosophical Quarterly, 1* (1964), 101–14.

Hobbes, Thomas, *Leviathan,* London, J. M. Dent & Sons, 1940.

Hook, Sidney, *Toward the Understanding of Karl Marx,* New York, The John Day Co., 1933.

Hospers, John, "Psychoanalysis and Free-Will," in Wilfrid Sellars and John Hospers, eds., *Readings in Ethical Theory,* New York, Appleton-Century-Crofts, 1952.

Kant, Immanuel, *Critique of Pure Reason,* trans. J. M. D. Meiklejohn, New York, P. F. Collier and Son, 1901.

Kneale, William, and Kneale, Martha, *The Development of Logic,* Oxford, Clarendon Press, 1962.

Lehrer, Keith, ed., *Freedom and Determinism,* New York, Random House, 1966.

Leibniz, Gottfried, *Theodicy, Essays on the Goodness of God, the Freedom of Man and the Origin of Evil,* trans. E. M. Huggard, Edinburgh and London, Routledge & Kegan Paul, Ltd., 1952.

Lewis, Clarence Irving, "A Pragmatic Conception of the *a Priori,*" in Herbert Feigl and Wilfrid Sellars, eds., *Readings in Philosophical Analysis.*

Lewis, Clarence Irving, and Langford, Cooper Harold, *Symbolic Logic,* New York, Dover Publications, Inc., 1959.

Linsky, Leonard, "Professor Donald Williams on Aristotle," *The Philosophical Review, 63* (1954), 250–52.

Lukasiewicz, Jan, "Philosophische Bemerkungen zu mehrwertigen Systemen des Aussagenkalkuls," *Comptes Rendus des Séances de la Société des Sciences et des Lettres de Varsovie (Sprawozdania z pozesieden Towarzystwa Naukowego Warszawskiego),* Classe III, Vol. XXIII (1930), Fascicule 1–3, pp. 51–77.

Maimonides, Moses, *The Guide For The Perplexed,* trans. M. Friedlander, London, George Routledge & Sons, Ltd., 1928.

Makepeace, Peter, "Fatalism and Ability, II," *Analysis, 23* (1962), 30–31.

Mates, Benson, *Stoic Logic,* Berkeley, University of California Press, 1961.

McCall, Storrs, "Temporal Flux," *American Philosophical Quarterly, 3* (1966), 270–81.

McTaggert, J. M. E., "The Unreality of Time," in *Philosophical Studies,* London, Edward Arnold & Co., 1934.

Morgenbesser, Sidney, and Walsh, James, eds., *Free Will,* Englewood Cliffs, N.J., Prentice-Hall, Inc., 1962.

Nagel, Ernest, *Logic Without Metaphysics,* Glencoe, Illinois, The Free Press, 1956.

Ockham, William, *Predestination, God's Foreknowledge, and Future Contingents,* trans. N. Kretzmann and M. McCord, University of Illinois, unpublished, copyrighted in 1964. The Latin original can be found as *The Tractatus De Praedestinatione Et De Praescientia Dei Et De Futuris Contingentibus,* ed. Philotheus Boehner, New York, Franciscan Institute Publications, 1945.

Pike, Nelson, "Divine Omniscience and Voluntary Action," *The Philosophical Review, 74* (1965), 33–34.

Plato, *Meno,* trans. Benjamin Jowett, New York, Library of Liberal Arts, 1957.

Prior, Arthur, *Time and Modality,* Oxford, Clarendon Press, 1957.

———, "Diodoran Modalities," *The Philosophical Quarterly, 5* (1955), 205–13.

———, "Diodorus and Modal Logic," *The Philosophical Quarterly, 8* (1958), 226–30.

———, *Formal Logic* (Oxford, Oxford University Press, 1962).

———, "Tense-Logic and the Continuity of Time," *Studia Logica, 13* (1962), 133–51.

Quine, Willard Van Orman, *Word and Object,* Cambridge, Mass., The M.I.T. Press, 1960.

———, *Elementary Logic,* rev. ed. New York, Harper & Row, 1965.

———, "On a So-Called Paradox," *Mind, 62* (1953), 65–67.

———, *From a Logical Point of View,* New York and Evanston, Harper & Row, 1953.

Rescher, Nicholas, *Studies in Arabic Logic,* Pittsburgh, University of Pittsburgh Press, 1963.

———, "A Version of the 'Master Argument' of Diodorus," *The Journal of Philosophy, 63* (1966), 438–45.

Ross, W. D., *Aristotle,* Cleveland and New York, The World Publishing Company, 1959.

Russell, Bertrand, *An Inquiry into Meaning and Truth,* London, Allen & Unwin, 1940.

———, *Our Knowledge of the External World,* London, Allen & Unwin, 1929.

———, *The Problems of Philosophy,* New York, Oxford University Press, 1959.

Ryle, Gilbert, *Dilemmas,* Cambridge, Cambridge University Press, 1954.

Saunders, John Turk, "A Sea Fight Tomorrow?" *The Philosophical Review, 67* (1960), 367–78.

———, "Professor Taylor on Fatalism," *Analysis, 23* (1962), 1–2.

————, "Fatalism and the Logic of 'Ability,' " *Analysis, 23* (1963), 24.

————, "Fatalism and Linguistic Reform," *Analysis, 23* (1962), 30–31.

————, "Fatalism and Ordinary Language," *The Journal of Philosophy, 62* (1965), 211–22.

Schleiermacher, Friedrich, *The Christian Faith,* ed. H. R. Mackintosh and J. S. Stewart, Edinburgh, T. and T. Clark, 1928.

Sellars, Wilfrid, and Hospers, John, eds., *Readings in Ethical Theory,* New York, Appleton-Century-Crofts, 1952.

Sharvy, Richard, "A Logical Error in Taylor's 'Fatalism,' " *Analysis, 23* (1963), 96.

————, "Tautology and Fatalism," *The Journal of Philosophy, 61* (1964), 293–95.

Skinner, B. F., *Science and Human Behavior,* New York, The Macmillan Co., 1953.

Spengler, Oswald, *The Decline of the West,* New York, Alfred A. Knopf, 1932.

Spinoza, Benedict De, *Ethics,* ed. James Gutmann, New York, Hafner Publishing Co., 1957.

Strang, Colin, "Aristotle and the Sea Battle," *Mind, 69* (1960), 447–65.

Taylor, Richard, *Metaphysics,* Englewood Cliffs, N.J., Prentice-Hall, Inc., 1963.

————, "The Problem of Future Contingencies," *The Philosophical Review, 66* (1957), 1–28.

————, "I Can," *The Philosophical Review, 69* (1960), 78–89, reprinted in Sidney Morgenbesser and James Walsh, eds., *Free Will,* Englewood Cliffs, N.J., Prentice-Hall, Inc., 1962.

————, "Fatalism," *The Philosophical Review, 71* (1962), 56–66.

————, "Fatalism and Ability," *Analysis, 24* (1962), 25–27.

————, "A Note on Fatalism," *The Philosophical Review, 72* (1963), 497–99.

————, "Comment," *The Journal of Philosophy, 61* (1964), 305–07.

————, "Prevention, Postvention, and the Will," in Keith

Lehrer, ed., *Freedom and Determinism,* New York, Random House, 1966.

The Holy Scriptures, Philadelphia, The Jewish Publication Society of America, 1941.

University of California Associates, "The Freedom of the Will," in Herbert Feigl and Wilfrid Sellars, eds., *Readings in Philosophical Analysis,* New York, Appleton-Century-Crofts, 1949.

Waismann, Friedrich, "How I See Philosophy," in A. J. Ayer, ed., *Logical Positivism,* Glencoe, Illinois, The Free Press, 1959.

Williams, Donald, "The Sea Fight Tomorrow," in P. Henle, H. M. Kallen, and S. K. Langer, eds., *Structure, Method and Meaning: Essays in honor of Henry M. Sheffer,* New York, Liberal Arts Press, 1951.

―――, "Professor Linsky on Aristotle," *The Philosophical Review, 63* (1954), 253–55.

Wilson, H. Van Rensselaer, "Causal Discontinuity in Fatalism and Indeterminism," *The Journal of Philosophy, 52* (1955), 70–72.

Zeller, Eduard, "Über den κυριεύων des Megarikers Diodorus," in *Kleine Schriften,* ed. Otto Leuze (Berlin, G. Reimers, 1910), *1.*

Index